THE WORLD
OF COGNAC

This edition published in North America in 1999
by Chartwell Books, Inc.
a Division of Book Sales, Inc.
118 Northfield Avenue
Edison, NJ 08837
© Copyright Paris 1997

designer: Sophie-Anne Sauvaigo
editor: Nicolas Jeanneau
translation: John Herrick
english language edition: Lisa Davidson
revision: Lise Aire

ISBN: 0-7858-1041-2
. Printed in Spain

THE WORLD OF COGNAC

GILBERT DELOS

Translated from the French by John Herrick

Photographs by
Matthieu Prier and Jean-Marc Lalier

CHARTWELL
BOOKS, INC.

FOREWORD

Cognac, supreme among the brandies of the world, owes its place of privilege not to any miracle of good fortune, nor to the unique climate or soil. Rather, it is due to the painstaking efforts of generations of men and women. Indeed, cognac stands as a testimony to man's ability to profit from the munificence of nature.

We can perhaps today identify the ingredients in the soil required to produce a Grande Champagne; we may be able to clone the vine of an ugni blanc, or copy to a "tee" a Charente still, but it is impossible to reproduce any of the cognacs in all of their aromatic diversity. This is because each cognac has its own identity, an identity that is unique to each particular brand. For the true secret of cognac resides in its history, a history that dates back over three and a half centuries and to which every individual involved in its production has made a personal contribution.

Cognac has survived the competition from other spirits, the blight of phylloxera and even the menace of taxation. The secret of its survival can be attributed to its versatility and its inexhaustible ability to satisfy the ever-changing tastes of the consumer. Whether served as an aperitif, as an after-dinner digestif, or as the perfect complement to a fine dinner, this versatile beverage has never ceased to please the imbiber from one generation to the next. This adaptability is due, ironically, to an unwavering adherence to age-old traditions. Born on the banks of a small river in France, cognac has become an emblem of status and a mark of good taste the world over. What follows will explain how that happened and perhaps why it is especially true today.

The supremacy of cognac is due above all to the tireless work of generations of men and women who, over time, have learned how to extract the best from nature.

CONTENTS

Born on the banks of a small river, little by little cognac conquered the world.

Once upon a time . . .

The original inventor of the world's most famous brandy will forever remain unknown, as will any precise knowledge of the exact date of this miraculous discovery. One thing seems sure, however: it is unlikely that the discovery of cognac can be attributed to any one individual. The cognac we know today is certainly the product of generations of winegrowers, distillers, and merchants.

That the Charente region proved to be the promised land of cognac is no accident. Indeed, it is the product of a combination of three key factors: climate, soil, and people. Only in the Charente can such a combination be found for the elaboration and exploitation of such a product. The soil is rich in chalk, and the climate is mild. The local culture also plays an important part. The inhabitants of the land are noted for their patience, determination, and business acumen. All of these ingredients are responsible for the quality of cognac and its worldwide success.

THE PIONEERS

The cultivation of the vine in Aunis and Saintonge dates to ancient times. These two provinces, along with Angoumois, make up the Charente region. A small vineyard was known to exist there already in Gallo-Roman times. The wine culture spread from the La Rochelle region from the twelfth century on, finally taking hold in the Cognac area over the next few centuries.

The locals were especially keen on the wine, but appreciation of the beverage spread as far as England, Flanders, and the Scandinavian countries. In the thirteenth century, a certain Henri d'Angély composed a poem entitled "The Battle of the Wines," in which he boasts about the wine from his native region. Henri pits the wine from Aunis against those of Moselle and Alsace:

Vineyards in Grande Champagne (left), and Charente-style stills (above), two symbols of the unique land of cognac.

You Alsace and Moselle
only the German tribes may souse
While I besot all England,
Brittany, Normandy, Flanders and Wales
Scotland, Ireland, Norway, and Denmark.
My borders extend so far
The greatest of Wines am I
showered in Kroner and Shillings.
(cited by Bruno Sépulchre in *The Book of Cognac*).

The fine quality of wine in those days, both red and white, only partly explains its international success. Merchants from Northern Europe had been familiar with the Charente region for quite some time because of its other famous industry: the production of salt, extracted from the salt marshes along the coast. At the time, salt was used as the universal preservative and was a sought-after and precious commodity. Due to the great demand for salt, merchants were willing to travel far and wide to procure it, and naturally this was their initial interest in the region. Salt introduced them to wine, which became a favorite product for export back to their native countries in the north.

Cognac thrived from its monopoly on salt, acquired in the twelfth century. Every shipment of salt had to pass through town. The salt tax was much lower in town than in the ports. And that is how a small town situated several dozen miles from the ocean became rich off salt from the sea.

Salt has left its mark indelibly on the town, for many of the old mansions built with money made on the salt trade are still standing today, such as the Gabelle mansion on the ancient rue Saulnier. However, the triumph of the wine trade remains apparent—the Gabelle mansion, for example, has long since been converted into a warehouse for cognac, as have many of the mansions in the old city.

The wines of Aunis and Saintonge have more than stood the test of time. They also survived the ravages of the Hundred Years' War, but suffered serious setbacks from competition coming from the Bordeaux region, which had a readily

accessible market after 1152: with the marriage of Eleanor of Aquitaine to Henry Plantagenet that year, Bordeaux came under the sovereignty of the English crown.

These close ties with Northern Europe would bring profound changes to the region. The people of the Charente had close business contacts with foreign merchants, and this early introduction to trade gave them a decisive advantage. This experience played a crucial role in the early exploitation of viticulture in the region and established the first pioneers

The stunning sight of a dolmen in the region of Charente.

of the cognac industry: men with the vision to foresee an extensive market and large profits. How important this factor is can easily be seen by comparing cognac to its older rival, armagnac. Both are excellent brandies, of equal and unparalleled quality, and yet armagnac is the lesser esteemed simply because it did not benefit from the extensive overseas ties that so handsomely promoted cognac.

More help came from King John Lackland, who in the beginning of the thirteenth century accorded Cognac a charter that gave it autonomy. This allowed the town to escape the effects of feudalism, and a powerful merchant class emerged. Nearby towns such as Jarnac, however, were not accorded this

privilege, which may explain why the region is today known as cognac rather than some other name like "Jarnac."

Cognac's good fortune would continue to grow. François I was born in the village and naturally, he favored the local merchants. Later, Louis XIV rewarded the town for its loyalty in resisting the princes of the Fronde by authorizing four different trade fairs each year. At the same time, Jarnac, Cognac's Protestant rival, was to suffer a series of setbacks.

A number of theories have been advanced to explain the proliferation of cognacs during the sixteenth century. One theory contends that the quality of wine at the time had seriously diminished, but no one can explain why. Another theory asserts that the rising cost of transportation obliged winegrowers to concentrate the wine by distilling it. Yet the emergence of cognac in Aunis and Saintonge remains an inexplicable mystery.

One thing remains certain, however: the Dutch, the masters of commerce at the time, played a crucial role in establishing the popularity of cognac. They were the first to industrialize the distilling process. Until then, spirits had been brewed by doctors and monks, then used to conserve the medicinal properties of herbs.

The Dutch were also intrepid voyagers, and spirits had the advantage over wine in that they were easier to preserve and so did not spoil easily during long journeys. Consequently the Dutch constructed large distilleries to meet the new demands for alcohol. Just as grain is stored in order to guarantee the future food supply of a population, the Dutch distilled and stocked large quantities of alcohol for commercial purposes. The most logical place to do this was at the point of commerce itself, which in this case was the Charente region.

The earliest evidence of the brandy trade in the Charente dates back to 1549. A merchant from La Rochelle purchased four barrels of quality brandy, as noted in a record from the period. The first known distiller was also from La Rochelle. A deed from 1571 mentions a certain Jehan Serazin, "merchant and maker of brandy." It wasn't until 1617, however, that the use of the term "cognac" was first mentioned in a sales contract, also by a merchant from La Rochelle. The first known distillery was created in 1624 at Tonnay-Charente by two Dutchmen.

The distillation process known as "charentaise" therefore owes little to the region itself. Curiously, about a century ago a legend sprang up that a certain knight named Jacques de La Croix-Maron invented the method. A real person by that name did indeed live in the area in the late sixteenth century, but historians have determined that he had nothing to do with the invention of the process.

Interestingly enough, the local people did not rush to capitalize on the new distilling methods. Not until the seventeenth century did it become a major activity for the people from the region, when the collapse of the wine trade throughout the area forced them into it. During a riot in 1636, the winegrowers of Cognac, Jarnac and Châteauneuf protested against the advantages enjoyed by their competitors from Aunis "who could sell wine more cheaply because of lower taxes, an economical location near the sea, and a monopoly on foreign trade. Consequently

the plaintiffs, to pay for the barrels and the production of the wine itself, had to sell their wine at unprofitable and vile prices so that it could only be distilled and converted into vinegar and brandy."

Distilling wine spirits was hardly a necessity until it became apparent that the end product largely exceeded in quality the raw material from which it was derived. By the middle of the century, London's high society ranked cognac among the most delectable wine products, as appreciated as port and wine from Bordeaux.

Another sign of the times for the burgeoning cognac industry was the introduction of a tax—the first of several—on the commodity in 1640.

The first cognac merchants appeared at this time: Ranson at Jarnac and Augier at Châteauneuf. These pioneers, probably in imitation of the Dutch example, devoted themselves not only to the production of brandy but also to the distribution and commerce of their product.

By the end of the seventeenth century, the cognac industry was firmly in place. It was due to the cultivation of grapes adapted for purposes of distillation, the proliferation of stills and above all the emergence of a mobile merchant class capable of selling it the world over.

THE MERCHANTS

By the beginning of the eighteenth century, the production of cognac had spread throughout the region, in particular Champagne, an area noted for its chalky soil where the best grapes are grown for distillation.

The reputation of cognac was soundly established. In 1726, in his *Memoires on the Angoumois*, Jean Gervais claimed that "the brandy from Cognac is indisputably the best in the world." Since such quality could not be attributed to the distillation process, which could be set up anywhere, it must have been due to the qualities of the soil and the vine. Soon, the local grape production was consecrated solely to the distillation of spirits, leaving drinking wines largely out of the picture.

Richard Hennessy, founder of the largest house of cognac.

The reputation of cognac grew steadily over the years as production became more and more intensive. The growing reputation naturally attracted the attention of foreigners, including the Dutch and especially the English. A motley crowd of disenfranchised younger sons and unemployed soldiers all migrated to the region to set themselves up in the cognac business. Among these characters were many Huguenots, political refugees fleeing religious persecution.

Their privileged relations with the Northern European countries, which had an unquenchable thirst for brandy, proved to be quite a boon. At a time when trading was both difficult and risky, the almost familial nature of trade relations made for a free, open, and secure commerce between the respective parties.

The Hennessy, Martell, and Hine families soon adopted French nationality and became respected and honored members of the community. The original patriarchs would eventually marry into the families of prominent local merchants in order to consolidate their fortunes. "He's become a son-in-law," it is said in Charente when referring to a foreigner who joins the company and goes on to assume control of the business.

The influx of foreigners continued unabated for some time. Soon to follow the Dutch and the British were Scandinavians, Germans, and even Russians. The people of Charente frankly acknowledge that this new blood was essential to the globalization of the cognac trade, a trade that from its very inception was of an international nature.

It required courage, if not downright audacity, to travel the globe in search of distant markets for cognac. Maritime travel in that era lasted for months, communication with the home port and intermediate ports was sparse, and the risks were great. Matters were further

were built on the banks of the Charente. The main means of transport over the centuries, this principal river was used to deliver the goods to port for shipping overseas. Special flat-bottom barges carried the cargo, and each barge was designed to ensure the security of the cargo while maximizing the potential load.

In the early days of cognac, the spirits were not allowed to mature for very long. Of course, the distillers knew that the longer the spirits were allowed to age in oak casks the better they became, but only a few distillers in Charente would reserve casks for long-term aging. Instead, most distillers were more preoccupied with

Trade with England was fraught with complications from the beginning, mostly because of the ancestral rivalry and repeated conflicts between the two nations. The French Revolution and, even more so, the reign of Napoleon resulted in a blockade that completely shut down official commerce between the two countries. This gave rise to vigorous smuggling operations, as well as large confiscations made by the British authorities. It is clear, however, that these operations were largely supported if not financed by the merchants themselves, who were eager to maintain supplies at a stable price. Consequently, the embargo had the favorable

Early twentieth-century grape harvest in the vineyards of Samuel Beau, near Segonzac in Charente.

complicated by political conflicts and unfair trade practices. Hardly anywhere in the world outside of Charente can merchants of such a vigorous and determined nature be found.

Richard Hennessy, for example, traveled to America to sign trade agreements with the newly created republic. And even though the Empire of Japan remained firmly closed to Western commerce, there were a few cracks through which the merchants of cognac managed to slip, and full commercial relations were opened up in the latter part of the nineteenth century.

At Cognac, as at Jarnac, the warehouses

sales than with quality, and they preferred to put the brandy on the market as soon as possible. Indeed, until the mid-nineteenth century, when the phylloxera blight hit the region, the custom was to maintain only minimal stocks covering no more than one year's worth of sales.

The client usually took responsibility for the aging process. Thus, for centuries, the London docks were used to store enormous stocks of cognac. The cold, dry atmosphere around the docks gave rise to a unique flavor called the "English taste," which still exists today in the Delamain cognac "Pale and Dry."

effect of increasing revenues on cognac sales by ensuring its scarcity in the face of rising demand.

The fall of Napoleon was warmly welcomed by the people of Charente, who were eager to resume the lucrative trade stymied by the enduring conflict. It is therefore somewhat surprising that after all the damage the Emperor had done to business in the region, he would one day become the namesake of a superior quality of cognac. Even more astonishing is the fact that this idea, the brainchild of two Englishmen (see Courvoisier), was so commercially successful in Britain.

In fact, the producers of cognac should have paid homage to Napoleon III rather than to his more famous uncle: it was during the Second Empire that cognac sales reached a zenith with a hitherto unprecedented popularity surrounding the brandy from Charente.

In the name of free trade, the period following 1860 saw halcyon days of lowered taxes and an expanding trade with Great Britain. Bottles of cognac were commonplace in almost every corner apothecary, cognac being prized as much for its medicinal properties as for its conviviality. Indeed, Martell was a leading supplier of cognac to British apothecaries.

Cognac sales continued to increase throughout the nineteenth century. The obvious success of cognac encouraged the manufacturing of counterfeit products. To protect their cognacs, merchants started branding each cask with an identifiable logo. Thus the "arm and axe" of the Hennessys and the stag of the Hines came into being, emblems often derived from the family coat of arms. Official brand-name registration began in 1856 under the authority of the Cognac chamber of commerce. Sixteen thousand different brands and companies have since been registered, a process that must be renewed every ten years.

Protection was further secured by the introduction of a revolutionary sales method: the bottle, which also changed production methods. Instead of selling the unaged brandy directly to the client, producers could deliver a finished product. This allowed them to decide to what extent it would be aged, which in turn allowed them to determine the cognac's eventual quality. Before that time, producers had little contol over their products, which were often blended with other spirits and sold at lesser prices.

Several decades went by before the bottle concept took hold. The oldest existing bottles of cognac date to 1850, but bottling may well have started earlier. The slow commercial response to bottling was due to the difficulty in obtaining enough bottles. They were handmade by

A loading dock on the Charente River. Until World War II, cognac was transported mainly by river boat.

glass blowers whose working conditions were abominable.

This situation improved thanks to Charles Boucher. Born in 1842, he was largely responsible for the innovations that improved methods of bottle production. He taught himself the craft as a child and went on to perfect a number of new techniques. In 1878, at the age of thirty-six, he moved to the Cognac region, where he invented a mechanical method for blowing and molding glass, which meant that inexpensive bottles could be produced on a large scale.

Important as the bottle was, it was overshadowed by a devastating event, the phylloxera blight, which laid waste to the vineyards of Charente. The disaster began in 1866 and did not abate until 1872. By then, the minuscule insect that caused the blight had wiped out the precious vines. With no means of combating the pest, winegrowers could do nothing but watch as their crops failed. Many were ruined and were forced to sell out their entire stocks to save what little remained.

The lesson was hard but it was well learned. From that time on, producers were punctilious in the handling of their stocks and started to oversee the aging process themselves. The consequence was a proliferation of different kinds of cognacs of a wider range of quality. This meant a greater sensitivity of the supplier to the type of the demand, with the elaboration of newer blends and production methods. The improving quality also resulted from greater competition, which made it important to distinguish one's own product from that of the competition.

The impact of the phylloxera debacle was complex. The devastated crops were replaced by American derivatives, but the winegrowers never recovered their former stature. New methods of cultivation were introduced that greatly improved productivity. The vines themselves changed, as the colombard and the folle blanche yielded to the ugni blanc and saint-émilion, which are more productive but less aromatic. These changes, of course, are the source of some nostalgia for connoisseurs who, in some cases, favor the pre-phylloxera (and extremely rare) cognacs for their specific aromas.

Despite the reconstituted stocks, cognac became increasingly scarce for several years. In some instances, producers were obliged to put substitutes on the market in place of the bona fide product. This led to the generalization of the term cognac, which today is often interchangeable with the generic term brandy. Indeed, in English-speaking countries, the two terms are even considered synonymous.

This "fraudulent" use of the word cognac has taken on phenomenal proportions. At the end of the last century, for example, it has been estimated that Italy was exporting fifty times more so-called cognac than it was importing. Germany

handsomely profited from abusing the cognac name. In addition to foreign brandy producers, other regions of France where brandies are produced also put up a fierce fight. Finally, the laws of 1905, 1909, 1919, 1929, 1935, and 1940 were enacted to protect each step in the manufacturing process (see the legal definition of cognac in the glossary on page 156).

The proliferation of counterfeit cognac stimulated the producers to find more varied means for distinguishing their products from those of their competitors. In 1907, for example, the Martell family

New labels and marketing schemes were also introduced, such as "End of the Century Mathusalem" or "Salvation Brandy," which showed a cannon shooting a cannonball shaped like a bottle of cognac. Other examples exploited the monarchy: "Honor to His Highness the Duc d'Orléans" and "La Françoyse, Grand liqueur de cognac created at the Court of François I," (though cognac didn't even exist then). The Boutelleau family had a hedonistic pitch: "A man needs four things to be happy: a pretty woman, a nice coffee, a good cigar, and

Publicizing cognac using Vercingetorix, the king of hearts . . . and Alexandre Dumas, shown here seemingly inspired with a glass of cognac in hand. Anything goes when extolling the wonders of cognac.

was also noted as being one of the largest producers of pseudo-cognac. However, this chicanery was not restricted just to foreign competitors, for even in the heart of the cognac-producing region several unscrupulous merchants had rented postal addresses with the sole intent of passing off their product as cognac.

The industry responded by trying to impose commercial control on the name of cognac as a guarantee of the product's true origin. The long, hard-fought battle lasted several decades, due to the strenuous opposition from those who had so

offered eight different varieties, each with a British name, as Britain was the largest consumer at the time. These were the X, XX, XXX, VO, VSO, VSOP, ESOP (aged forty years in its cask) and the Extra (aged fifty years). The shape of the bottles varied as well, with each one given its own unique form to target a specific type of clientele.

A number of curiosities also appeared during this period of frenetic diversification, including blends that contained a small amount of cognac or fine champagne with such frivolous appellations as "Le Coup de Jarnac" or "Brandy Bark."

most importantly, a glass of fine Boutelleau cognac." Even serious artists were conscripted into the cause with such talents as Cappiello, Jean d'Ylen, and Mucha, contributing to add a touch of class to the labels.

THE MULTINATIONALS

Cognac went global during the twentieth century, largely due to its universal popularity and an ever-expanding market. Ironically, the volume of production increased only moderately: from 1951 to 1960, average production was 49 million bottles a year, whereas in 1881, the figure stood at 63 million—significantly less than the 107 million bottles produced in 1878, before the effects of phylloxera were felt.

The challenge in the twentieth century has been to replace markets that disappeared, such as the United States during Prohibition; Russia, lost in 1917; and China, lost in 1949. Nevertheless, new strategies, and the children of Jarnac and Cognac were sent overseas to mind the family businesses. As recounted by Jean Monnier in his memoirs as chief of operations and head of the house of cognac founded by his father: "If business sent us to Singapore or New York, that was hardly thought of either as a privilege or a problem. It was part of the business and a simple case of necessity."

A plain advertisement found in Jarnac for the house of Dor bears testimony to this irrepressible desire to seek out and conquer new markets. In color and large print it advertises the line of cognacs it sold in Chile during the last century—with the address of the local distributor clearly on display. It is hard to imagine the enormous efforts that must have been required in order to make cognac a profitable enterprise in such a distant country.

Although political upheavals affected production, the calm and quiet lifestyle in the towns of Charente was hardly disturbed during either of the two world wars, aside from the normal restrictions on commerce that occur during such conflicts. In fact, it was during the interwar period that matters got difficult for the cognac producers, due to the increasing tax rates in France and rising duties imposed on imports by other countries. Hennessy and Martell took the matter in hand and divided the principal international markets between themselves and fixed their prices to discourage any competition from producers of the less expensive brands.

The German occupation, likewise, had little effect on the cognac trade. Otto Klaebisch, the German authority in Charente, knew the region well and came from the Meukow family of cognac producers,

1945. The tranquil, idyllic life of the people of Charente was hardly disturbed by the two world wars.

whose business was confiscated in 1914. The local merchants were obliged to cede enormous quantities of cognac to the occupiers, but the Germans were more than willing to pay a good price for it. Foreign exports, however, notably to Great Britain, were reduced to practically nothing. Consequently, the producers accumulated large stocks of aged cognac. Merchants and growers cooperated to increase stocks on a scale not seen since after the phylloxera blight.

The postwar period was marked by a startling change for the worse in cognac sales. All that was to change in the 1960s, when the market recovered and a boom in production levels occurred. Indeed, the average annual volume of production exceeded—for the first time in nearly one hundred years—the levels enjoyed prior

In Shanghai, as is true throughout the Far East, cognac is a favorite.

to the phylloxera blight. Record production levels were reached in 1973 with 257 million bottles. Exports accounted for most of this figure, with worldwide sales still exceeding ninety percent of the total supply. Since the 1990s, the proportion of bottles sold for export has continued to increase, while consumption in France itself has been in steady decline.

This gigantic surge in production has been accompanied by a change in the overall quality of cognac. The "Trois Étoiles," which for a long time comprised the bulk of sales, has been giving up more ground to its commercial rival, whisky, which is less expensive and widely promoted by a more diverse group of distributors. On the other hand, VSOP and the XO, for

example, have grown in popularity, consistent with the image of cognac as an elitist beverage and a sign of distinction and good taste. Rémy Martin seized upon the trend and has invested much in augmenting its sales of Fine Champagne.

This explosion in production and sales has had numerous consequences. The traditional structure of the different cognac businesses has changed drastically. Once family-owned business have now become increasingly dominated by large multinationals. This was inevitable as family funds dried up with financing acquisitions and maintaining stocks. This was in part due to the family legacies themselves, which divided the capital between the respective heirs and heiresses from

generation to generation. This failure to concentrate capital made the families vulnerable to takeovers by outsiders, who had long been eyeing the ever-increasing profits made from cognac. Thus Courvoisier, Bisquit, Hennessy, and Martell each lost financial independence, while smaller houses were either absorbed or eliminated. The larger brands benefited from these mergers by developing a global market and diversifying into champagne, whisky, porto, and gin.

The people of Charente finally lost control over their businesses, and the decisions are now made in offices in New York, Paris, and London. The link between the land and the people who profit from it has grown ever more tenuous, resulting in the inherent problems in maintaining the product's quality and authenticity. Commercially, the image of cognac has suffered. The trend has been to sell not just a single high-quality product but to bombard the consumer with a whole line of spirits, pushing those that are easiest to sell. The strategy that had made cognac one of the world's most preferred alcoholic beverages has been abandoned by the commercial behemoths, leaving, nevertheless, a niche for others: smaller brands such as Gourmel, Dor, and Fussigny have succeeded in maintaining the authentic, aromatic qualities that attest to a cognac's true origins and its traditional links to the land.

Another consequence is that the growers are no longer anonymous. They used to sell brandy and nondistilled wine to middlemen, but have pooled their capital to accumulate stocks of old cognac. A number of growers have even formed cooperatives, some of them quite large, with names like Unicoop (under the brand name of Prince Hubert de Polignac). Others have decided to go it alone and develop their commercial interests independently.

This movement has had its greatest impact on the Grande and Petite Champagne, symbols of quality and excellence, whose sales have soared. Tourism has played a significant role in the selling of these exclusive products, and today the roads of Charente bristle with billboards and advertisements inviting the passerby to sample the local goods. Concurrently, many of these producers are also developing trade contacts in Hong Kong or San Francisco.

The growth of cognac sales seemed endless, but some limits were reached in the 1980s. Of course, the gigantic Chinese market opened up after the political changes in the late 1980s. Other markets, however, stagnated. Competition from whiskey battered cognac at this time and challenged its reputation as the sole emblem of quality and good taste. An overall drop in the consumption of alcohol also depressed sales significantly.

Bottling is done today on a production line.

Not surprisingly, stocks of cognac increased in consequence and in some cases represented as much as six years' worth of sales. These reversals are not entirely unfortunate since the vintages affected were for the most part of an inferior quality, such as the Bois Ordinaires. Though the productivity of the vine had increased appreciably since the phylloxera blight, overall yields of brandy were restricted by interprofessional agreements and production quotas. Beyond a certain volume of production, wine is not allowed to be distilled as brandy, but as industrial alcohol. An offshoot of these limitations has been an increased volume of the nondistilled wine products from the region.

Following years of intensive production, producers are returning to the traditional methods which emphasized the qualities derived specifically from the land. Instead of trying to compete with whisky and other alcoholic beverages—which are less dependent on the climates and lands of their origins—cognac is promoting itself for its unique regional characteristics.

Will producers and merchants be willing to abandon mass production, including that of cognac meant for the Chinese markets? They must realize that consumer demand has evolved in favor of a cognac that is ever more expressive of the land and ever more unique and perfect in its appeal. It is here, where individuality is the stamp of excellence, that cognac has no peer . . . and no competitor.

An advertisement from a Hennessy ad campaign targeting the enormous Asian market.

The art of cognac

The ancient alchemists designated "quintessence" as the fifth essence, a subtle and ethereal substance. This term fits cognac most suitably, for the making of cognac requires no fewer than the four elements of earth, air, water, and fire, and cognac is their completion, their "quintessence." Indeed, it is the earth of Charente, the grapes and the wine it produces, the climate of the region, the distillation of the wine, and the effects of aging which perform the alchemy that goes into the making of cognac.

THE LAND

If the scientific classification of the different kinds of land of Charente occurred only during the last half of the last century, it has been known from the beginning that the soil played a crucial role in the quality of cognac. By the early eighteenth century, the area around Segonzac was called Grande Champagne for the excellence of its products.

The secret of the land is the presence of chalk in the soil. The thicker the layer of chalk underlying the earth, the flakier it is, a crucial property for growing the right grapes for cognac. The chalk not only adds a particular flavor to the grapes, it also creates an underground reservoir for the rain that falls on the region, so the vine has plenty of water during the dry, hot days of summer. Clay can also serve this purpose. In the Borderies region, also well known, there is a large amount of clay that regulates the water content of the soil.

The Grande Champagne, which produces the most famous cognac, is in fact composed of an entire chalk basin, called the "bassin campanien," "campanien" being the Latin cognate from which the term "Champagne" is derived. Some parts of the region are so rich in chalk that the topsoil is hardly present (or nonexistent altogether) so that the chalk is exposed and in full view.

The farther one strays from the Champagne region, the more compact the chalk becomes until it is almost watertight. Mixed in with the chalk is clay, and this has the effect of making the vines particularly sensitive to the climate.

The classification of the land had an uneven history before the final classification denominated six different Charente zones (see box at right). A few of these original designations were even somewhat frivolous, mainly as a result of the merchants' marketing techniques. Thus, a certain house of Barbezieux published in 1890 a "menu of wine producers" in which only four vintages are mentioned, while the existence of Segonzac, known at the time as the capital of Grande Champagne, was entirely ignored.

The geologist Coquand was the first to produce an acceptable scientific classification of the lands. This study was published in 1858. Coquand was accompanied on his research by a connoisseur who was responsible for verifying the quality of each cognac produced from the respective lands. Other scientists, among them Lacroix, completed this research,

Cognac: land and know-how.

THE SIX *DIFFERENT AREAS OF CHARENTE*

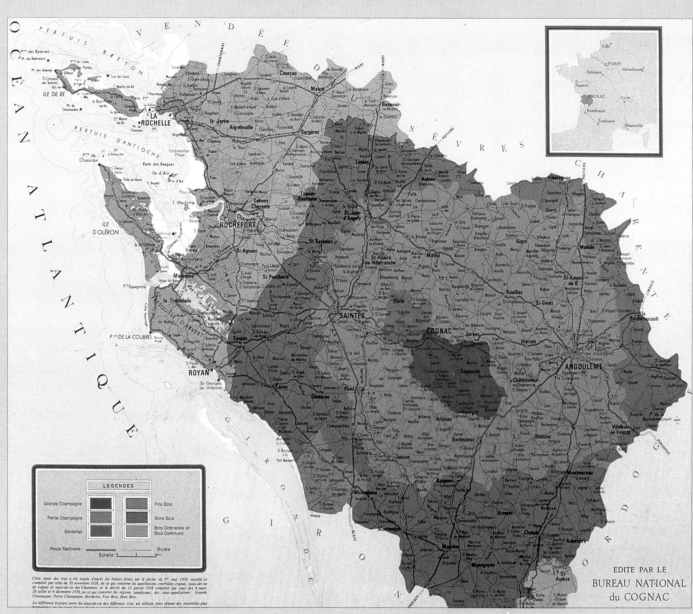

Before the phylloxera blight, the vineyards of cognac covered over 691,600 acres. Today only 215,633 remain, of which 204,089 are devoted to the production of the white wines used in making cognac (1992 figures).

Grande Champagne: 33,409 acres of land, south of the village of Cognac in the Charente region. These grapes are most prized for the quality of the cognac they produce, as it ages well.

Petite Champagne: 39,567 acres of land, which encircle the Grande Champagne region. It is slightly less appreciated than the Grande Champagne. Fine Champagne consists of a 50-50 blend of Grande Champagne and Petite Champagne.

Borderies: the vineyards cover 10,196 acres situated northeast of

the village of Cognac. This vintage yields a florid cognac that is very aromatic and characteristic of the Martell style.

Fins Bois: 84,975 acres, which surround the preceding zones. It accounts for about 40 percent of the total cognac production. The quality of these cognacs varies considerably.

Bons Bois: 31,791 acres, which surround Fins Bois. The quality of the cognac is noticeably inferior to those of the other vineyards and is marked by its heaviness.

Bois Ordinaires: 4150 acres, which produce a lesser quality cognac. The land is situated essentially to the west, in the region around La Rochelle and Rochefort. Production in this region is on the wane, much to the regret of the locals.

and final classification was officially established in 1938, though the actual work had been done by 1910.

The idea of a *cru* for cognac is completely different from that used to characterize Bordeaux wines. It does not imply a hierarchy in the quality of the respective products. According to the BNIC *(Bureau national interprofessionel du cognac)*, the term is merely used to identify which cognacs are which and what territories they come from.

This partitioning by name has been a point of contention since the classification of 1938. The issue at stake concerns

Ugni blanc is the principal grape in making cognac.

the attribution of the appellation cognac to regions extending into the Charente-Maritime *département* and even into the islands of Ré and Oléron. The expansion in the brandy trade in the 1960s and 1970s has been lamented by critics who claim it has vitiated the name of cognac.

THE VINE AND THE WINE
The culture of wine in the Saintonge region dates to the Gallo-Roman era, but its true origins date from the Middle Ages, following the marriage of Eleanor of Aquitaine and Henry Plantagenet. This marriage brought the region under the dominion of the English crown.

One of the first varieties of vine used for growing grapes for distillation was the balzac. Next was the folle blanche, a vine that produced an incredibly aromatic cognac. It was the ravages of phylloxera that forced the growers to turn to another variety, the ugni blanc, also called saint-émilion. Today, this variety accounts for almost all the grapes used for distilling cognac. Traces of colombard and folle blanche account for the rest.

All of these varieties, with the exception of colombard, are Mediterranean in origin. The rigors of winter in the Charente region significantly stunt the growth of these vines and they never reach full maturity by the time of the harvest.

This, however, is exactly what the growers and distillers want. The people of Charente discovered early on that the more acidic the wine, the less alcoholic it is, which is just what is needed for distilling an excellent brandy. So the notion that the wine of Charente is only good for distilling brandy because it is otherwise undrinkable is not at all accurate. On the contrary, the whole point is to produce a wine that does not exceed ten percent alcohol by volume and that is low in sugar content. Of course, this does not make for a very drinkable wine, but again this is not its purpose. It is the same situation with champagne.

Phylloxera changed the variety of grape used in making cognac, and had an enormous impact on the methods used for cultivating the vines. Prior to phylloxera, the vines were grown low to the ground and bunched together rather than high above the ground and in rows, as is done today. The difference is a notable increase in the yield of grapes and an overall mechanization of the growing process. The harvest tractors have improved efficiency significantly, but at a cost—oil leaked onto the grapes often ruins the flavor of the cognac. Still, today up to eighty percent of the grapes are harvested mechanically.

Though their methods of cultivation may differ from other wine-producing regions, the people of Charente are just as scrupulous in caring for their vines as any other winegrower. For example, the person in charge of the vines at Frapin, one of the larger vineyards, personally oversees the growth cycle and takes samples of the leaves and vine shoots and replants them following trituration.

Phylloxera may today be nothing more than a bad memory, but the vines still face a number of different potential blights. For example, eutypiosis has spread rapidly in recent years, with as much as forty percent of the vines affected in 1992, compared with only eighteen percent in 1982. This disease causes the vine to rot for reasons that are still poorly understood. The BNIC has been studying this problem intensively for the last few decades and their specialists are pursuing research into the causes and effects of this disease.

Yet the yield from the vines has continued to increase. In 1940, one hectare (2.47 acres) of vines produced three hectoliters (79.2 gallons) of pure alcohol, whereas in 1992 the volume produced was 10.3 hectoliters (272 gallons). The amount of production that is allowed for wine-based goods has been limited by quotas. The surplus alcohol is sold for industrial uses.

The harvest usually takes place about a month following the Bordelais harvest. The wine is fermented rapidly over a few weeks and is then ready to be distilled.

DISTILLATION

Distillation takes place once the fermentation period is over. Distillation occurs in a still according to the "charente method," which involves double-distilling the wine.

Following fermentation, the wine is first separated from the dregs, though some distillers prefer to leave them mixed in with the wine during distillation. Then the wine is transferred to the boiler or pot where it is heated. Boiling concentrates the alcohol in a liquid form called the *brouillis,* which is about twenty-seven to thirty-two percent alcohol by volume and represents approximately one-third of the initial volume of wine. The process is repeated two more times and then a

For a long time, wood was the only fuel used to heat the stills.

second distillation, the *bonne chauffe* (literally "good warming") takes place. The vapors released by the second distillation are concentrated in the head which sits above the boiler. This passes into what is called the "swan's neck" before it finally

condenses in the serpentine, kept cool by a bath of cold water. The result is pure brandy, which must not exceed seventy-two percent alcohol by volume in order to qualify for use in making cognac.

The experience and expertise of the distiller is called upon at two critical steps: at the start of the process and at the end of the step called the *bonne chauffe.* At these two points in the process the alcohol contains undesirable elements. The most important thing is to determine when the *coeur de chauffe* (or distillate) must be selected. Alcometers constantly register the percentage of alcohol, and thermometers carefully regulate the heat required to yield the perfect distillation, but the distiller is indispensable, since he knows certain details, such as the wine's acidity and its initial alcohol content. Successful distillation depends on just such experience.

Every stage in the distillation and production of cognac is rigorously regulated by law. For example, the size of the still is

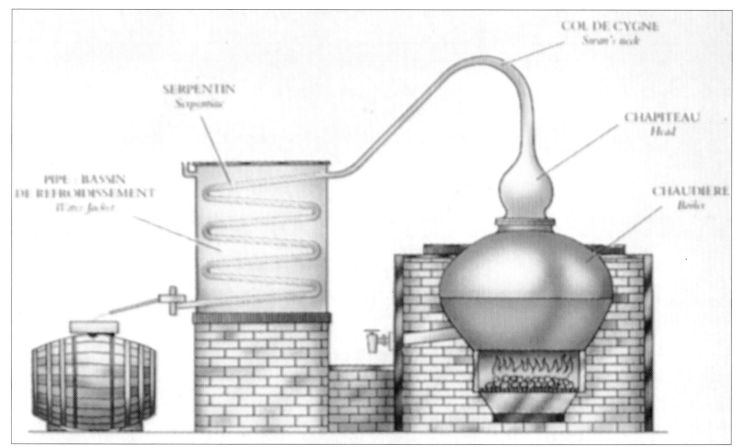

SERPENTIN
Serpentine

PIPE : BASSIN
DE REFROIDISSEMENT
Water Jacket

COL DE CYGNE
Swan's neck

CHAPITEAU
Head

CHAUDIÈRE
Boiler

A Charente still.

As it leaves the still, the brandy is clear and must not exceed 72% alcohol by volume.

not to exceed 792 gallons, which limits the total volume to be distilled at any one time to 660 gallons. The larger the still, the more neutral the brandy. There is one exception to this rule: the boiler used to obtain the *brouillis* can contain up to 3,696 gallons, for 31.7 gallons of wine.

The pot must be heated by an open fire. Today, gas is used almost exclusively, while in the past, wood was the primary source of energy (before coal was used). The use of gas has freed distillers from the responsibility of spending the night watching the fires, replenishing the fuel every two to three hours for several weeks at a time. In the past, ingenious methods were developed to awaken the distiller when the fire needed tending. One such method used a wax-coated thread attached at one end to a tankard and at the other to the swan's neck. When the wax melted the tankard fell onto the pot and the resulting noise would wake up the distiller so that he could recharge the furnace. Today, more modern conveniences do the job.

Though the principles involved in distilling brandy have not changed over the centuries, the still has undergone a number of important modifications. A lot of research has gone into improving the head that tops the boiler. Its role is crucial, since it collects the alcoholic vapors while preventing the boiling liquid from entering the swan's neck. At first it had a rather rectilinear shape until it took on the more curved form known as "the Moor's head," the conduit that connects the bulge at the base of the swan's neck to the serpentine. Its shape has evolved progressively from century to century, from an olive shape to the now familiar, optimal onion shape. This change in shape may have resulted in the loss of some of the more personal aspects characterizing the various cognacs, but its overall effect has been positive, leading to a general improvement in the quality of the final product.

The wine heater is another innovation and one that is more recent. It was invented in the middle of the nineteenth century. Its purpose is to economize on energy. The idea is simple. The swan's neck enters the reservoir containing the wine to be distilled. Next, the wine is heated to the right temperature required for its distillation. Improper use of this device can result in an oxidation of the wine with adverse consequences for the quality of the distillate. Consequently, the wine heater is not generally used and the house of Martell expressly prohibits it.

The stills used in Charente for distilling cognac are exclusively made of copper. Other less expensive alloys have been tried and rejected as inadequate. Moreover, the process of double-distillation

Only copper is allowed in making a Charente still.

Chestnut wood straps are often used to protect the oak casks when they are moved.

has proven to be essential for obtaining the maximum amount of flavor and aroma, despite the fact that cheaper methods are available for distilling cognac.

The process of distillation must, by law, be finished by the end of March. As a result, the distillers must work day and night from the time of the harvest. This regulation also has the practical purpose of limiting the fermentation of the wine over a period that does not extend into spring. Too long a fermentation period has adverse consequences for the characteristics of the wine that are essential to distilling a fine cognac.

There are about three thousand stills in Charente and about half of them belong to private distillers who produce cognac on a relatively small scale. The other half belongs to the large, professional companies and established houses of cognac.

AGING COGNAC

Once the distillation has been completed, the production of cognac enters the final and perhaps most mysterious stage: the aging process.

The young brandy, fresh from the stills, is immediately placed in new oak casks, made of wood from the forests of Tronçais in Alliers, or from the Limousin. The casks are then stored in *chais* called *jaune d'or* (or ground-level storage cellars), which get their name from the official certificate. By law, these *chais* are used only for stocking and aging cognac.

The fabrication of the casks is something of an art in itself. The oak trees used must be 150 to 180 years old. They are cut down, then partitioned into planks and split, never sawed so that the wood fiber is not cut lengthwise (which affects the watertightness of the cask). The freshly

cut cask-wood, called *merrains,* is then stocked in the open air for at least five years. Exposing them to the changing seasons aids in drying them out. Artificial methods, such as kiln-drying, have been tried, but the cognac did not age properly.

The finished *merrains* are then used as staves, which are assembled by the cooper to make the cask. The staves are fitted together using metal hoops and the seams between the staves are progressively sealed by squeezing them together with the aid of steel wires. The staves are assembled around a brassero, which heats the interior of the cask. The wood is constantly humidified so that it does not split while being shaped. When finished, the cask is placed upright and the staves are cut evenly to form the top. The finished cask is then secured with strips of chestnut wood so that it can be rolled without damaging the cask. It takes a skilled cooper an entire day to make a cask.

Once the bung is cut, the cask is washed and placed in a water bath for two to three days. Then the cask, which can hold 80 to 105 gallons, is ready for the cognac.

Inside the cask, the wood transforms the alcohol over a series of three stages. The first stage lasts about a year and is known as "extraction." Hydrolysis and degradation processes take place over a second period lasting one to two years. The third and final stage is the most complex, and involves an oxidation process.

During this stage—and sometimes earlier—the new cask is replaced by a cask that has already been used. These are called *roux,* or red casks. They imbue the cognac with less tannin, but allow for a more harmonious aging to occur.

The maturation of cognac involves a delicate exchange between the wood, the brandy, and the oxygen in the air. The volume of cognac inside the cask diminishes some two to three percent each year, a loss poetically referred to in Charente as the "angel's portion." The brandy is steeped in the tannin and different aromas, notably vanilla, while the process gradually darkens the cognac. The glycerines rot slowly, which also adds to the distinct characteristics of cognac.

The evaporating alcoholic vapors stimulate the growth of a fungus called the torula, which proliferates on the walls and ceilings of the *chais* where the casks are stocked. This fungus causes the characteristic black puddles of run-off that can be seen all around Cognac and Jarnac, evidence of the nearby presence of a *chai* where cognac is being aged.

Every element contributes to this slow transformation. To begin with, the wood must be carefully selected. Oak from Limousin, hard and coarse grained, is adequately porous and contains some of the most favored tannins. Oak from the forest of Tronçais, originally planted by Colbert for constructing ships for the navy, is softer and has a finer grain. This oak requires a longer period of aging and results in a less woody cognac. Clearly,

An entire day is needed to make an oak cask.

the choice of wood has a profound effect on unique style of each house of cognac.

The type of *chai* is also of crucial importance because the ambient temperature and humidity will influence the rate at which the cognac ages. The cellar master must regularly modify both its temperature and humidity to obtain the desired result. Incidently, the first *chais* were built along the Charente River, and the constant humidity from the river played a vital role in the flavor of the cognac at that time.

Today, the *chais* are spread all over the Cognac region and often rely on natural methods of humidifying the casks, such as the collection of rainwater. A controlled humidity prevents the cognac from becoming too strong, and this is verified by the cellar master by a sampling from the casks in each *chai* once or twice a year. This poses a formidable challenge to the master and his mates, given that they are few in number while the number of casks to be sampled can reach into the hundreds of thousands. For Yann Fillioux and his band of merry men at the house of Hennessy, one might agree that they have their work cut out for them.

The brandy must be aged three years before it officially becomes cognac and can be sold as such. The average amount of time spent in the cask is, of course, considerably longer—in some cases, up to fifty years. Beyond that limit, nothing more is gained and the cognac begins to turn. If the cognac is of exceptionally high quality, it is transferred into glass demijohns or very old casks that no longer contain tannin. No further aging takes place, but the decades that have gone into the production of the cognac will be preserved indefinitely.

BLENDING COGNAC

It is at times possible to find cognac that comes from a single cask, but these varieties are extremely rare and represent a minuscule proportion of the commercial product. Usually, they can be obtained directly from the distiller only.

As with champagne, the full expression of a cognac comes only after it is cut or blended with other cognacs. The term "cut" is perhaps misleading since it suggests that the cognac is blended with other substances or alcohols, which is strictly forbidden.

Blending consists in joining different cognacs from different locales to create a unique flavor reflecting the individual tastes and preferences of the merchant or producer. It is the cellar master who ensures the cognac's unique flavor. This job requires years of experience and perhaps thousands of tastings each year.

The cellar master, not surprisingly, is a breed apart in the world of cognac. His sense of cognac is worth a bundle to the producers. The most remarkable example

> ## THE AGE OF COGNAC
>
> No cognac is allowed to be sold as such if it has not been aged for at least two and a half years, starting from the first of October of the harvest year. The age of a cognac is determined by the youngest brandy making up the blend.
> The only legitimate classifications are the following:
> Trois Étoiles or VS (Very Superior): cognac that has been aged less than four and a half years.
> VSOP (Very Superior Old Pale), VO (Very Old), Réserve: cognac that has been aged between four and a half and six and a half years.
> Napoleon, XO, Extra, Hors d'Âge: cognac that is more than six and a half years old.
> All other indications of age are not controlled by the BNIC and are guaranteed only by the producer and/or seller.
> The use of a vintage year is authorized only under very strict conditions, which makes such cognacs very rare.

is perhaps the Fillioux family. For over seven generations, a Fillioux has been in charge of quality control for Hennessy, the very first merchants of cognac.

In addition to providing to the product with its unique qualities, blending diminishes the alcoholic content of the cognac, which is usually sold at forty and sometimes forty-five percent alcohol by volume. It would take forty to fifty years for this reduction in alcohol to occur by unaided evaporation, which would price the product out of range. The cellar master is therefore obliged to dilute the cognac with distilled water. Some producers find this method lacking in subtlety and prefer more delicate measures, such as adding titrated mixtures of cognac and water to maintain the balance of the blended product. These mixtures are around twenty percent by volume and

are themselves aged several months prior to use. This is the way it is done at Delamain, where every aspect of production is carefully monitored to achieve the right effect.

Aside from water, other additives are used to enhance the aromatic and alcoholic qualities. Wood shavings, for example, are added in the belief that this accelerates the aging of the cognac. Molasses or caramel is also often added. Restrictions limit the sugar added to the brandy to an amount not exceeding two volumes per thousand. This practice, not universally appreciated by cognac lovers, darkens the color of the cognac.

These darker cognacs are largely sold on the Southeast Asian market, where lighter cognacs are considered to be of an inferior quality. In Britain, a diametrically opposed opinion prevails.

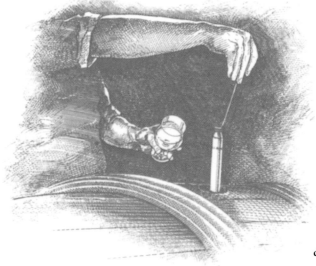

The cognac sampler is essential during tastings.

ALL ABOUT COGNAC

It is all thanks to the Dutch that the brandy known as cognac gained its reputation as an excellent export product. Cognac was so successful that it attracted the attention of merchants from England, Ireland, Germany, and even Scandinavia and Russia. For the most part, these foreign adventurers would in time become as Charentais as the Charentais themselves, and many went on to assume important social and political functions in the region. The Englishman Otard, for example, became mayor of Cognac and held the office for almost twenty years.

Make no mistake, however: One or two centuries ago, it was not so easy to move to Charente, set up a business, and export overseas a couple of casks of cognac. Keep in mind that the labels and bottles presented in the following pages tell the stories and lives of the men, and in a few rare cases, women, who ventured forth in the cognac trade. The only reassurance they had as they began their conquest of the spirits world was their confidence in what was unquestionably the best brandy in the world.

Of course, let's not forget the talent and patience of the winegrowers, distillers, and cellar masters. Still, the real adventure of cognac is best expressed by the merchants who were undaunted by the rigors of traveling from Moscow and Singapore. May the multinationals who have taken over these noble institutions never forget the example set by the intrepid men and women who once steered cognac over the perilous seas of world trade.

A vineyard in Charente, including the *chais* used for aging cognac (left). Above: a fresco depicting a harvest in Charente.

Edmond Audry

MERCHANT
SAINTES (CHARENTE-MARITIME)
1878

This small and discreet house of cognac is not well known, but that doesn't stop the connoisseurs from appreciating the quality of its cognac. This quality can be attributed in part to the very old *chais* in which the cognac is aged.

Augier

MERCHANT
COGNAC (CHARENTE)
1643

This oldest of the houses of cognac is the last of the original establishments that originated the cognac trade. Its survival is largely due to its ownership by Mumm, which maintains a relatively low profile as far as its cognac is concerned.

Its founder, Philippe Augier of Châteauneuf, was a merchant in the larger sense of the term, cognac being only one of the many commodities in which he traded. Under his direction, and later under the direction of the Augier family, the house of Augier Frères rapidly became one of the largest cognac producers in the region. Their reputation as clever and serious businessmen was unparalleled. The name of Étienne Augier is perhaps best known historically for the fact that he married into the Martell family. Elected deputy of the "Constituante," he stood in favor of the Royalists and was rewarded for his allegiance with a barony during the Restoration.

The Bournonville and Varenne families assumed control of the house through their earlier alliance with the founder, Philippe, and continued its activities. This occurred at the time that the Martell and Hennessy families began to surpass Augier in sales of cognac.

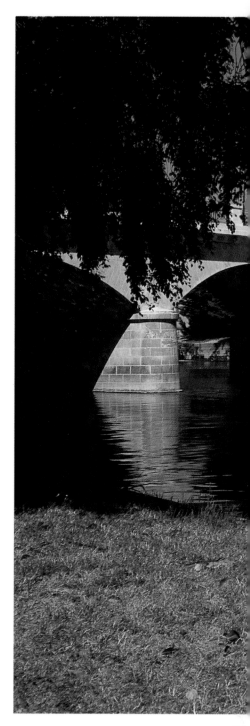

The old town of Cognac with the main bridge over the Charente.

At the end of the 1960s, Sam Bronfman, head of Seagram's, the world's largest spirits merchant, became interested in acquiring a house of cognac. His idea was to repeat the success he had with Chivas Regal, a blend of fine whiskies.

He cut a deal with Jacques de Varenne in 1968 with the intention of buying up Augier's cognac stock.

The death of Sam Bronfman shortly afterward, however, cut short the proposed projects, and the stock was resold by Bronfman's successors when enthusiasm for the idea waned. Twenty years elapsed before Seagram's was to show interest in cognac again, and in 1988 the company acquired Martell.

Michel Amart

WINEGROWER-DISTILLER
**DOMAINE DE LIZET,
SAINT-MARTIN-D'ARY
(CHARENTE-MARITIME)**

The land is located in the most southern part of the Charente-Maritime, in Bons Bois. The company has belonged to the

Amart family for three generations. They also own the Jean Faure winery of Saint-Émilion. Forty-two acres of vineyards produce the grapes used in making white wine and cognac, which is distilled at the winery in a modern still holding 660 gallons. The brandy is aged in casks newly constructed from Limousin oak, then transferred to older casks for storage. Amart produces a pineau des Charentes, as well as Trois Étoiles and VSOP cognac.

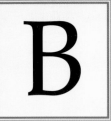

Banchereau

WINEGROWER–DISTILLER
ÉRAVILLE (CHARENTE)
1968

Daniel Banchereau inherited fifty-seven acres of Grande Champagne vineyards in 1968. At the same time, he decided to enter the cognac and spirits trade. In 1991, with his children Frédérique and Laurent, he moved into the distilling business. Today, the family distills and sells a line of cognacs and two pineaux des Charentes. Christened Mon Cognac, the line relies on a feminine aspect in its promotional approach. For example, there is the Rendez-vous, a VS-based cocktail, and the equally persuasive Complicité, made with an Hors-d'Âge from Grande Champagne.

Paul Beau

WINEGROWER–DISTILLER
SEGONZAC (CHARENTE)
AROUND 1890

The house was founded by Samuel Beau and relies on 247 acres of Grande Champagne vineyards. The buildings and tools are all original, dating from the time of the founding of the house, and, according to the present directors, are still in

use. After the death of Samuel Beau shortly before the outbreak of world war I, his son Paul assumed control and immediately set about improving the aging methods. Though the company originally produced only cognac, Paul Beau decided in 1977 to involve the company more directly in the selling of its own goods.

The line includes only exceptional cognacs such as the Vieille Réserve, aged 12 to 15 years, with an alcohol content of 40%. There is also the Hors d'Âge, aged between 20 and 25 years, with an alcohol content of 43%, sold in a bottle with a slightly twisted neck. The Borderies Extra Vieilles contains 44% alcohol by volume, and is a perfect example of what proper aging can do for a cognac from Grande Champagne.

One of Bertrand's stills.

Bertrand

WINEGROWER-DISTILLER
Réaux (Charente-Maritime)
1731

The Bertrand family has been cultivating the same 173 acres of land, known as the Brissons de Laage, since 1731. The vineyards are located in the Petite Champagne area.

The cognacs of Bertrand have been widely commercialized since the end of the last century. In 1905 and 1907, they were awarded prizes at expositions in Liège and Bordeaux. Currently under the control of Raymond Bertrand and his sons, the house sells only Petites Fines Champagnes in accordance with the usual categories. It also sells a variety of pineaux des Charentes, which are aged over a long period in oak casks.

The founder, Alexandre Bisquit.

Bisquit

WINEGROWER-DISTILLER-MERCHANT
Jarnac, later Rouillac (Charente)
1819

In 1819, when he was barely twenty years old, Alexandre Bisquit established his own cognac outlet in Jarnac on the banks of the Charente River. A great adventurer (he traveled as far as China to sell his products), he was nevertheless very attached to his home town. A staunch republican, he became mayor of Jarnac during the revolution of 1848 and remained in office until the arrival of Napoleon III. He was at first associated with a certain Trioche and later entered into partnership with Adrien Dubouché, his son-in-law. Dubouché was above all a painter and potter, and he established a museum of ceramics at Limoges. This may explain why the image of Saint Martial, first bishop of Limoges, adorns the labels of the bottles and is featured in advertisments for Bisquit-Dubouché.

As has often happened in the cognac trade, a son-in-law, Maurice Laporte, assumed control of the business in 1865 after marrying Solange, Adrien Dubouché's daughter. Like his grandfather by marriage, he would go on to become mayor of Jarnac and even a senator. The descendants of Laporte-Dubouché sold the family business in 1965 to Paul Ricard, who, riding high on his success selling pastis, had developed an interest in the cognac trade. He made a substantial investment in this new venture, moving the business from Jarnac after he purchased a superb estate, the Château de Lignières, north of Rouillac. This property

had for a long time been in the possession of Rémy Martin. Beyond the 494 acres of Fins Bois vineyards, the company also boasts the largest distillery in all of Charente. No fewer than fifty-six stills are at work at Lignières, where Bisquit also maintains its own cooperage. The château itself is a wonderful place surrounded by a beautiful park with trees over one hundred years old. Its twenty luxury rooms and a renowned chef make it the perfect venue for receiving and entertaining international figures and important clients.

In 1991, Bisquit again expanded when it acquired Castillon-Renault. The company has since been known under the name of Renault-Bisquit. Founded in 1835 at Cognac by Jean-Antoine Renault, Castillon-Renault was a well-known innovator in the business and one of the first to export cognac in bottles.

Despite major investments and management by Pernod-Ricard (founded in 1974), Bisquit has never overcome the competition of the bigger houses of cognac. For years, the company produced the Trois Étoiles class of cognac which today is known as the Classique. Their strategy has since changed and the line now has two categories with two different types of bottles. They are:

• The Diamant bottle, something like a VSOP. It is aged 8 to 10 years. The Prestige, a Fine Champagne, is aged 12 years, and the Napoleon, which is a 20-year-old Fine Champagne.

• The Diamant carafe with a glass stopper, which includes the XO Excellence, a Fine Champagne aged 30 to 35 years, and the Extra, a Grande Champagne aged 50 years.

• Lastly, there is the Privilège d'Alexandre Bisquit. Presented in a special bottle, this is a blend of more than 80 Grande Champagne cognacs dating from 1878 to 1914. Bisquit also maintains a collection of cognacs, some of which date back to 1819, the year the house was founded.

Brillet

WINEGROWER-DISTILLER
LES AIREAUX AT GRAVES (CHARENTE)
1850

Guy Brillet, the founder of this cognac house, was born at Bois-d'Angeac in 1656. For over ten generations, a family member has run the company. Today, it is run by Jean-Louis Brillet. Originally small winegrowers and distillers, the Brillet family gradually expanded their estate in the Grande Champagne and Petite Champagne areas.

In 1850, Vivien Brillet (sixth generation) moved the family business to Aireaux in the area of Graves alongside the Charente River. He developed the estate (173 acres of vineyards in all), founded the distillery and built the *chais*. Between the two world wars, Raymond and then Jean Brillet (eighth and ninth generations) were among the first to bottle and sell pineau des Charentes, although most of their cognac was destined for the shops.

In 1985, Jean-Louis Brillet decided to involve himself more directly in the commercialization of their products and he came up with the idea of the *cru* and proposed for the first time the Single Cru as a denomination. He inherited his ancestors' sense of caution, and like them, reserves a good third of his production for stock. The cognacs are distilled in a small still (396 gallons) and are aged up to fifty years in oak casks and then transferred to demijohns.

The line clearly reflects the origin of the cognacs: Petite Champagne for the Sélection (aged 5 years) and the Réserve (aged 10 years), and a Grande Champagne for the Grande Réserve (aged 10 to 12 years), the Très Vieille Réserve (aged 18 to 20 years), and finally the Héritage. This last cognac is aged 50 years and contains 45% alcohol by volume. Also on offer is the Très Rare Réserve Limitée, containing 40 to 42% alcohol and blended with a number of brandies, some of which date to the beginning of the century (80 years old or more). These last two are sold in hand-blown glass bottles, capped with black wax and numbered. Brillet also sells a number of remarkable pineaus, which are aged with the dregs for at least two years prior to bottling.

Michel Bureau

WINEGROWER-DISTILLER
LE GRAND LANDRY AT GUIMPS
(CHARENTE)
1893

These vineyards were created in the Grande Champagne area between Archiac and Berbezieux in 1893 by Victor Albert and distillation began in 1914. The sons-in-law later took control of the business. Alphonse Bobin initially assumed control; Michel Bureau, who gave his name to the brand, followed. Today, his sons François and Jean-Luc are in charge.

In the classic cognac tradition, Bureau sells several qualities of cognac made from Petite Champagne grapes: Trois Étoiles, VSOP, Vieille Réserve and XO in a carafe (introduced in 1993, it is a blend of cognacs aged over 30 years.) The line also has some pineaus (including a white pineau aged 15 years in the cask), a variety of cognac-based liqueurs, different wines, and a sparkling wine: the Cave du Père Albert.

Camus

WINEGROWER-DISTILLER-MERCHANT
COGNAC (CHARENTE)
1863

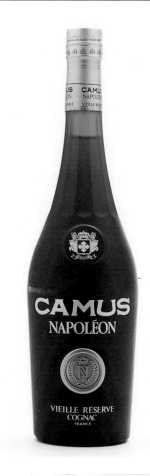

Camus is the fifth-largest producer of cognac and the largest independent producer. The house has had much success — but also some remarkable setbacks — since its inception in 1863. The family tradition is very much a part of the operation, as Jean-Paul Camus, the man in charge today, asserts: "There is nothing easier than making cognac. All you need is a father, a grandfather, and a great-grandfather, to do it right."

Jean-Baptiste Camus, the founder (1828-1898), was a winegrower who moved to seventy-four acres of land in the Borderies area at Plessis. Initially, he distilled cognac for sale to other merchants before deciding to go into the commercial side of the trade himself. In order to obtain the necessary stocks, he allied himself with several other winegrowers and created the brand La Grande Marque.

Success came quickly. In 1870, more than seven thousand casks of Fine Champagne were sold in London. Jean-Baptiste then turned his attention to the Russian market.

In 1890, he bought out his partners and became the sole proprietor of Camus-La Grande Marque. His sons Edmond and Gaston followed him into the family business and helped to expand operations throughout France and overseas. Gaston was the most active in overseas affairs and regularly visited Saint-Petersburg, where he hunted bear with Czar Nicholas II.

THE RUSSIAN MARKET

The Russian Revolution of 1917 slammed the door shut on the enormous Russian market with near-devastating consequences for the house of Camus.

Moreover, huge quantities of exported merchandise were never paid for, leaving the future of the company in doubt. Seven daughters were born to Gaston and Edmond before the arrival of Michel in 1911. Much was expected of Michel, but he had other ideas and decided upon a career in medicine instead. In order to change his mind, his father locked him in his room for several days and then expedited him to Great Britain to teach the boy a lesson in the cognac trade and family duty.

Michel finally succeeded his persuasive father in 1932 and inherited a sizable load of problems, since the company was still far from recovering from the loss of the Russian market. He launched an aggressive marketing campaign in France, which accounted for forty percent of all cognac sales at the time. The idea was to associate the name of Camus with Henri IV through the nickname "verre galant," literally "gallant glass," a pun on Henri IV's nickname of "Vert Galant." He also

concocted the idea of cognac and soda in order to counter the menace arising from the increasing popularity of whisky.

In 1959, Michel Camus finally managed to redress the situation with Russia. An accord was reached between Camus and the Soviet Union, which allowed the company to sell its wines and spirits there in exchange for exporting Soviet goods to France.

It was during a trip to Asia that Michel Camus had the insight that would finally

The porcelain flagons shaped like books have made Camus a hit in duty-free shops in the Far East.

37

restore the company to its former glory. He discovered the first duty-free shops and developed an appreciation for Asian (especially Japanese) taste and the stylistic presentation of high-quality products.

One more ingredient went into the works. He hit on the idea of exploiting Napoleon's two-hundredth birthday to promote his goods. A new brand of cognac in a book-shaped bottle was introduced. This form was chosen because, like a book, it was easy to slip into a suitcase. It was made of fine white Limoges porcelain, sported the bust of Napoleon, and was adorned with a variety of decorations.

Its success in Asia was immediate, and four years later, a new version with a different color was introduced. There were to be ten in total over the years following Camus' observation of the Japanese fetish for collecting cognac bottles.

The book form would be used to promote other goods with variations on the original theme. Thus, one bottle celebrated the marriage of Prince Charles, and another the bicentennial of the French Revolution, and even works by famous painters such as Van Gogh and Renoir were featured on the bottles.

The market targeted by these bottles required a fairly rapid turnover in the types of packaging used. This resulted in a new function at Camus involving three specialists whose duty it is to seek out and implement new ideas for bottles and to assess their potential on the Asian market. One came up with the concept of Lover's Rings, a porcelain carafe displaying interlaced rings on its cap. It has been a huge success among Japanese newlyweds who traditionally spend their honeymoons abroad, giving them plenty of opportunity to pick up a bottle in one of the airport duty-free shops.

Camus' consumption of porcelain as a packaging device accounts for up to ten percent of the total porcelain production from Limoges.

GOING IT ALONE

Michel Camus would eventually turn over control of the business to his two sons, even though the company experienced impressive growth in the 1970s. Philippe was in charge of the French market, and prior to that, he had been mainly involved in a company engaged in distributing spirits—Camus France Distribution, now defunct.

Jean-Paul was mainly involved in export and pursued his father's success in the duty-free business. He has also involved sports as a means of promoting the goods, a practice unheard of in the cognac business until then. It began with the 1978 World Cup in Argentina and has since included figure skating, hot-air ballooning, and horses as a means of selling Camus.

However, it is in defending its independence that Camus has invested the bulk of its efforts, and has succeeded so far in resisting the trend by which other

Jean-Baptiste Camus, the founder.

Chabanneau

DISTILLER-MERCHANT
COGNAC (CHARENTE)

This brand is only one of many introduced by CGEVF *(Compagnie des grandes eaux-de-vie de France)*, which is directed by Jack Germain-Robin. The line includes not only different cognacs (ranging from VS to XO) but also pineaux des Charentes, armagnacs, calvados, and assorted other brandies. This makes for a total production volume of 6 million bottles a year, bringing in 160 million francs in 1994 alone. Ninety-five percent of the production is destined for export to some 140 different countries. How much of that is cognac is not specified.

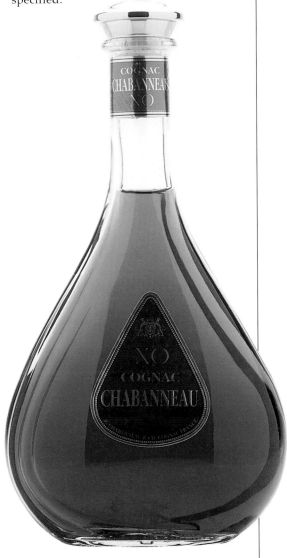

houses of cognac have become subsidiaries of multinational companies. A winegrower in his own right, who personally owns three vineyards in Broderies and rises each morning among his own vines, Jean-Paul Camus maintains close social and economic ties with the winegrowers who supply him with the raw materials for making his cognac. This interest is best exemplified by Camus' publication of the winegrowing review *Contact,* which includes important information on the techniques of growing grapes and making cognac, in addition to providing market analyses and details on the company's activities.

Today, the Camus group employs two hundred people and owns 49 acres of vineyards in the Grand Champagne (château d'Uffaut) area and 309 acres in the Borderies. Four distilleries, at La Nérolle, Longchamp, Lorignac, and Saint-Laurent-de-Cognac, employ forty-four different stills, representing a production volume of 7.9 million gallons of brandy.

The group acquired new *chais* for aging the cognac at the beginning of the 1990s. These are located at Merpins, near Cognac, and are built according to the traditional Charente style of rubble stone walls and tiled roofs. The humidity required for the proper aging of the cognac is assured by a system of pipes that channels rainwater throughout the building and principally along the base of the walls.

Camus exports its cognac to 140 different countries, and places emphasis on the production of aged cognac: fifty-five percent of production is Napoleon, XO and Extra, while only thirty-five percent is VSOP and just ten percent is Trois Étoiles.

In addition to the traditional line, Camus also offers a number of special products such as the carafe Jubilee, which is irregularly shaped, and the Michel Camus in a bottle made of Baccarat crystal.

The family tradition continues at Camus with Jean-Paul's sons: Jean-Baptiste and Cyril, who are being groomed to one day assume control of the family business.

The two herons of Chabasse.

Chabasse

MERCHANT
SAINT-JEAN-D'ANGÉLY
(CHARENTE-MARITIME)
1818

Almost unknown to the public until now, Chabasse cognac made a splash in 1993 and earned recognition not only for the impeccable assortment of products it offers but also for the originality of the bottle designs and the

cognacs used in its blends. The Chabasse family has longstanding links to the cognac trade dating back almost two centuries. Son of a *gabarier* (*gabares,* or flat-bottom barges, were used to transport merchandise up and down the Charente River), Jean-Baptiste Chabasse was born in 1778 and later went on to specialize in the brandy trade. In 1818, he founded his own business in the region of Saint-Jean-d'Angély. Little by little, he acquired a vast collection of vineyards and turned eventually to the business of distilling cognac from wine purchased from other growers. An almost larger-than-life character, he also became the local mayor. He lived to age eighty-five, and at his death he left his four sons an estate of more than 1,976 acres, which is an enormous piece of land for the Charente region. He also left them with a lucrative business in distilling and trading in bulk.

His sons, however, had substantially less character. The estate was divided up following the phylloxera blight and the business side of matters experienced a number of setbacks. Louis-Olivier Chabasse, however, made something of a name for himself as a result of his travels to the Far East at the beginning of the century.

René-Luc Chabasse, belonging to the fifth generation, pursued

Chabasse uses blends of cognacs from Petite Champagne and Fins Bois.

Denis Charpentier

MERCHANT
ANGEAC-CHAMPAGNE (CHARENTE)
1984

Denis Charpentier came onto the scene in the 1980s as a wine merchant. His company, UNEXPA, soon turned toward the cognac trade and has focused primarily on exports to the Far East, in particular China, and the extensive duty-free network throughout Asia. Charpentier's cognacs are made mainly from Fine and

the wholesale trade and had little interest in selling individual bottles of cognac. He changed his mind about that at the beginning of the 1990s when the market for cognac was booming. And so the brand name Chabasse was born. His strategy was to concentrate on the better-quality cognacs using a modern approach. The blends used are only Petite Champagne and Fins Bois, while the bottles are impeccably but simply shaped. The most innovative bottles, used for XO and XO Imperial, were awarded the Oscar for packaging in 1995. In the same simple style, there is a Baccarat carafe. René-Luc

Chabasse has recently introduced a second line of cognacs christened Bowen. The line pays homage to Elisabeth Bowen, who ran a farm near Madras in India and who met Louis-Olivier Chabasse during one of his voyages. The cognacs making up this line are more characterized by Broderies grapes, and the packaging is more masculine in its appeal. A leather girdle encircles the base of the bottle, which also has been received favorably by the public, winning an Oscar for packaging and a Prix Verre-Avenir in 1996. The Bowen line offers a VSOP, Napoleon, XO, and Extra.

Grande Champagne grapes and have enjoyed considerable success, winning a number of international prizes, which in turn helped to boost sales. The line includes for the most part a VSOP, a Napoleon, an XO, and an Extra.

Along with cognac, the company also sells another brandy (produced outside of the Cognac region) under the brand name Robert Loston, demonstrating its obvious intentions of entering the market for other spirits. The target again is the worldwide network of duty-free stores.

Courvoisier

DISTILLER-MERCHANT
JARNAC (CHARENTE)
1835

Courvoisier owes its reputation to the innovation of a new class of cognac dubbed Napoleon. The brand fancies that its orgins extend back to the Emperor, which is believable given a few judicious and imaginative historical interpretations…

Its founder, Émile Courvoisier, was partners in the early nineteenth century with Louis Gallois, who opened one of the first wine and spirits outlets at Bercy. An engraving from 1811, now on display at the Carnavalet Museum, depicts Napoleon I "visiting the Gallois outlet," based on speculation that the business furnished Napoleon himself with wine and spirits.

Other anecdotal evidence helps to fuel the fires of imagination. In July of 1815, Napoleon, in deep trouble, sought refuge aboard a ship based at Rochefort and bound for the Americas with a cargo of brandy on board.

Napoleon ultimately decided to stay in France. When the ship was later intercepted by the British Navy, the sailors, finding only cognac on board, supposedly christened it "Napoleon's Brandy," such was their appreciation of the Emperor's good taste. Yet the term Napoleon was not registered until a century after that purported event.

Indeed, history is much more drab than legend. The house of Courvoisier was created in 1835. Félix Joseph Courvoisier, the son of Émile, set himself up in Jarnac and entered the cognac trade to keep the family outlets supplied with brandy. In 1855, he went into business with his nephews, the Curlier brothers. Courvoisier, like other houses of cognac, prospered during the Second Empire. In 1860, Courvoisier became the personal supplier to the British royal family.

Félix Joseph Courvoisier left no descendants when he died in 1866, and

Napoleon made a fortune for
Courvoisier... in Great Britain!

the business fell under the control of the Curlier family. Napoleon cognac still did not exist: it was the idea of two Englishmen, Guy and George Simon, who bought the company in 1909. They were the descendants of a French Protestant family exiled centuries earlier to Britain. Shrewd businessman, they saw a great opportunity in the historic enmity between England and the Empire, and launched the new cognac classification of Napoleon.

COGNAC NAPOLEON

Nevertheless, it wasn't an original idea. Other than the labels bearing the imperial coat of arms (especially those of the Second Empire), the idea was already overused: Bisquit launched in 1890 its First Consul Cognac with a portrait of Napoleon, and Meukow in 1899 introduced its Cognac Grande Champagne-Marque Napoleon with a mention of the "1812 Harvest."

The Simons deserve the credit for the Napoleon marketing pitch, a phenomenal success in Britain. Rather than a full portrait, they displayed only a silhouette with the caption "The Brandy of Napoleon." Courvoisier later introduced a dark green, frosted glass bottle, which became the signature of the line. The term "Napoleon" then developed into a new class of cognac that is considered superior to the VSOP.

During World War II, Courvoisier was singled out for special treatment by the German occupiers, largely due to its English origins. The German occupation in France soon created serious financial difficulties for the company. Business continued, however, under the control of George Hubert and Christian Braastad, a ploy that did not prevent the Germans from sequestering the company in 1942. After the Liberation, business was better than ever, thanks to the enduring appeal of the Napoleon name.

With operations set up in a château in the heart of Jarnac, Courvoisier underwent a period of rapid growth that was almost too fast for its own good. As a result, the company fell victim to its habit of short-term planning. Its preference was to purchase what was needed on the spot rather than to develop substantial stocks of its own. This was in part due to its intense activity on the local market, as well as in the area of export, which was part of the director Christian Braastad's strategy of maintaining a strong presence in France. The uncontrolled escalation of sales and prices in the 1960s was too much for the company; unable to finance new acquisitions, the company found itself in dire financial straits. A number of merchants were interested in Courvoisier, but it was the Canadian group Hiram Walker, already a cognac distributor in the United States, that finally bought up the company in 1964. That same year, Courvoisier became one of the four largest cognac producers in the region.

The "Napoleon obsession" continues—Courvoisier has acquired Napoleonic relics, such as the Emperor's personal effects, his famous hat, coat, and tent he used during his campaigns, all now on display in the company museum in Jarnac.

The company has also continued to innovate. After introducing a special kind of bottle dubbed the "Joséphine," the company has developed such new technologies as the micro-distillation of wine and an elaborate plumbing system for filling and draining casks.

The winds of change that govern international commerce have resulted in new ownership of the company. In 1986, Allied-Lyons, later to become Allied Domecq, a British concern, succeeded Hiram Walker as Courvoisier's overseer without altering the products themselves. Today,

The *paradis* at the house of Courvoisier.

sales reach up to 1.2 million cases a year of which ninety-seven percent is destined for export. The company maintains two distilleries and works under contract with 1,200 winegrowers and 300 other distillers. Stock in 1994 reached the equivalent of 86 million bottles, most of it

Napoleon, an honorary society, is meant to exalt the most prodigious foreign promoters of French spirits and gastronomy. But Courvoisier, dedicated to the image of the Emperor, did not stop at the use of the effigy alone. In 1988, the company called upon the talents of Erté, the decorator and painter of Russian origin who specialized in the Art Déco style. He was to help launch a new line of cognac, christened the Collection Erté. A special carafe was designed for its promotions, decorated with a series of original designs: Vine, Grape Harvest, Distillation, Aging, and Tasting. A new model of carafe was released each year in a limited edition (12,000 bottles each time); each bottle contained a selection of old brandies from the Grande Champagne area, the oldest of which dates to 1892—the year of Erté's birth.

The success of this line has been remarkable, especially on the foreign markets. In Singapore, for example, a Vine bottle sold

for 31,000 francs at auction. Despite the death of Erté in 1990, the collection survives—seven designs in all and each the creation of the artist.

Another attempt at snob appeal has been the company's attempt to commercialize 595 bottles of Succession J.L., the initials of a Grande Champagne winegrower who was known for having once sold a shipment of very old and prestigious cognac. Packaged in numbered bottles and sealed in eighteen-carat gold, this cognac is sold in a handmade wooden box. A certificate of sales signed by a broker and a bailiff guarantees the authenticity of each bottle. That might justify the price of 24,000 francs a bottle the buyer must shell out for such a rarity.

Label designed by Erté for the cognacs of Courvoisier.

stored in the company's enormous warehouse, visible from all points in Jarnac and as you enter the town.

The classic line in the so-called Joséphine bottle includes the Trois Étoiles, the VSOP, and the Napoleon. Next, in more luxurious bottles, is the XO, and the Initiale Extra made from Borderies and Grande Champagne grapes, without a distinction in age. The Ordre de

Croizet

WINEGROWER-DISTILLER-MERCHANT
SAINT-MÊME-LES-CARRIÈRES (CHARENTE)
1805

In the seventeenth century, the Croizet family formed a renowned vineyard in Grande Champagne at Saint-Même-les-Carrières, and in Fins Bois at Champmillon, where they distilled their own cognac. In 1805, Léon Croizet decided to go

into the business of selling cognac. He worked to combat the phylloxera blight by surrounding his vineyards with stone walls. The idea, which was to protect the vines that had been grafted onto healthy American plants, earned him the Légion d'Honneur. In 1892, the estate was taken over by J. Eymard, the husband of one of

Croizet's daughters who received a dowry of a stock of the finest cognacs, which has been preserved. Philippe Eymard, of the sixth generation, is the current director of one of the oldest independent and family-owned distillers and merchants of cognac in the world.

Croizet possesses a vast estate with properties in Flaville, eighty-nine acres; Couronnes de Douvesse, eighty-nine acres; Maine-Androux, forty-four acres; and the château de l'Épine, for about 430,000 vines, yielding a production volume of more than 264,000 gallons. Croizet also owns distilleries, *chais* for aging and storage, and shipping operations. As its name indicates in French, Saint-Même-les-Carrières has long been the site of an important quarry for the stone used to build the châteaux and buildings of the Charente region. Today, there remains an enormous underground network of galleries and chambers covering a total of some nine miles. In the past, Croizet took advantage of the caverns to age its cognac. They were suited perfectly to that task due to the constant temperature and humidity. This practice was abandoned, however, because of the risk of cave-ins. Croizet holds several gold medals for the outstanding quality of its cognacs, and has further benefited from a network of 120 representatives. Its efforts have largely been confined to the production of top of the line cognacs. The brand is featured in a number of famous restaurants such as Troisgros, Bocuse, and La Tour d'Argent.

The Croizet line of cognacs offers a Trois Étoiles, a VSOP, a Napoleon, and an XO (age not specified) and also a 50-year-old cognac. It should be noted that Croizet is one of the very rare houses to offer special vintages under the name of Récolte and sold in numbered bottles. The oldest, Lot 33, is a cognac over one hundred years old. The origins of these special vintages is guaranteed by the company.

The Croizet family at the beginning of the century. Pierre Croizet supplied different merchants for many years, but began selling his own cognac in the 1970s.

Pierre Croizet

WINEGROWER-DISTILLER-MERCHANT
LANTIN (CHARENTE)
1793

The Croizets have been winegrowers in the region since the early seventeenth century, near Jarnac on the right bank of the Charente River in Fins Bois. They began distilling in 1793 after purchasing a still for twenty gold louis, quite a sum at the time. For many years, the Croizet family distilled only for local merchants, notably Hennessy and Martell, while maintaining their own personal reserves of aged cognacs.

In the 1970s, the family decided to start selling their own cognacs, principally for export, which was booming at the time. The line today includes a Trois Étoiles, aged four years; a VSOP, aged seven years; a Napoleon, aged fifteen years, sold in a Cognac or Norman bottle; an XO, aged twenty-five years, in a Cognac bottle or a carafe; and the Extra Extra, aged thirty-five years, sold in a carafe. Finally, the Excellence, aged fifty years and sold in a cracked-varnish bottle capped with a wax seal, has achieved celebrity status on the Asian markets.

Davidoff

MERCHANT

Davidoff cognacs were created by two men. Zino Davidoff was born in 1906 into a family already rich in the experience of blending and selling fine tobaccos of the Orient. He then made fine cigars, first from Cuba and then with tobaccos from the Dominican Republic and other areas of the Caribbean. When Kilian Hennessy was born, his family had been distilling and trading in fine cognacs since 1765.

Both men were devoted to quality and to the idea that a superb cigar and an exceptional cognac make a perfect partnership. Davidoff cognacs are the only ones that Hennessy blends and bottles for any firm other than Hennessy itself. Davidoff cognacs thus benefit from the huge reserves of eaux-de-vie aging in the Hennessy *chais* in Cognac, and also from the group LVMH (Louis Vuitton-Moët-Hennessy), a world leader in the luxury goods market. Davidoff produces two labels:

• The Classic, which is a blend of about forty eaux-de-vie from Grande and Petite Champagne, Borderies, and Fins Bois, the oldest of which are some twenty years old. They are aged principally in new oak casks, which gives a structured bouquet of oak, vanilla and honey. Dark amber in color, its aromas of vanilla and oak are followed by fragrances of forest undergrowth and old roses. The texture is round and the flavor persistent, with evidence of long aging appearing in the intense flavors of honey and vanilla.

• The Extra, a complex blend of old brandies from the finest growths, some over forty years in age. Once blended, the cognac is then aged for an additional eighteen months to harmonize its components.

It is bottled at forty-three percent alcohol by volume. An intense aroma of oak is followed by perfumes of burnt orange and old leather. Its rich and unctuous flavors linger on the palate like those of the fine cigar it is meant to accompany.

Delamain

MERCHANT
JARNAC (CHARENTE)
1824

This cognac is considered by the experts to be the standard against which all others are measured. Delamain owes its reputation to scrupulous attention to details. Exclusively a merchant house, it has proven that the key is in the aging and blending.

Nicholas Delamain left Saintonge in 1625 with Henriette-Marie de France when she married Charles I of England. A Protestant, he chose to stay in England, but a descendant, James Delamain, went to France in 1759 and entered the cognac trade in 1763, in partnership with his father-in-law, Isaac Ranson, member of an old Cognac merchant family. But their business went into liquidation in 1817.

In 1824, Henry, James' grandson, went into business with his cousins, the Roullets. This lasted until 1920, when the Delamain family assumed sole control. After World War II, Alain Braastad, whose mother was a Delamain, became co-director with his cousin Patrick Peyrelongue, also grandson of a Delamain.

The family is illustrious not only for its cognac. Philippe (1849-1902) was a famous archaeologist. Of his three sons, Robert became director of the business and in 1935 published a still authoritative history of cognac; Jacques introduced modern ornithology to France, and Maurice was co-owner and director of the publishing house Stock. Jean, Jacques's son, was a leading specialist on wild orchids.

The Delamain operation at Jarnac is modest, in contrast to many other ostentatious installations. The offices are in an ordinary house, and the *chais* and ateliers are in other discreet buildings.

THE DELAMAIN PRINCIPLES

Delamain shuns marketing ploys. Its cognacs are intended as the fullest expression of the Charente soil and the fulfill-

ment of the house's distilling and aging techniques. Delamain cognacs rely on craftsmanship and several principles:

• All of the brandies are from Grande Champagne and are by the best distillers.

• No contract binds the house to its suppliers. Each purchase is preceded by a thorough sampling. Long-term suppliers are familiar with the house's standards, but the house is constantly seeking others who can meet its demands.

• The use of new oak casks is prohibited to avoid excessive tannins. Aging is done in older "red" casks kept in *chais* next to the Charente River.

• The reduction of the alcohol level to forty percent is achieved over months by slowly adding diluted brandies of fifteen percent alcohol.

• Each cognac is aged individually prior to blending, so as not to disrupt the different ages and styles of the brandies used.

• After blending, the final product is aged an additional two years.

• The final coloring is minimal, and only to ensure a homogeneity of color.

Demijohns containing the oldest cognacs of the house of Delamain.

Concentrating on top-of-the-line cognacs (which account for only 10% of total production), Delamain offers a fairly restricted selection.

Only three of its cognacs are distributed internationally:

• Pale & Dry. Created in the 1920s, it is the most "English" of the Delamain cognacs. It is aged anywhere from 22 to 28 years and is delicate and light. It is both floral and mellow, with a nuance of vanilla. The name indicates the difference. "Pale" rather than "brown," the term used to designate those cognacs darkened by the addition of molasses. "Dry" is used to distinguish this cognac from the many sweeter varieties. In 1966, Delamain redesigned the bottle. The metal thread that once surrounded the bottle during the period when the bottles were not mechanically capped has been abandoned.

• Grande Champagne Vesper, aged on average 35 to 40 years. It was introduced in the 1950s. More in line with classical cognac, the color is somewhat dark with a superb golden tint. It is the perfect digestif, a marvelous after-dinner companion. This mellow and round cognac has a complex aromatic effect on the palate that is nevertheless very subtle. The label displays an engraving from 1790 showing a scene at a cognac *chai*.

• Très Vénérable Cognac de Grande Champagne, has an average age of 55 years—the maximum time a cognac can be aged in a wood cask. It is in fact a very old Pale & Dry, of an amber-topaz color. Its freshness is as unexpected as its balance and aromatic variety. The play on the palate is magnificent.

• Réserve de Famille. A cognac for more personal consumption, it is made today from a brandy that comes from Saint-Preuil in the Grande Champagne area that was distilled before the last war. Stored and transported in a demijohn, the natural unreduced alcohol content of this cognac (42%) has been maintained during storage. It is a marvel in its own right, and the Delamain family essentially reserves it for their friends and closest clients.

• Vintage. Delamain is one of the few houses that has the right to sell vintage cognacs. In 1962, it was decided, in effect, not to authorize the commercialization of this denomination, since legislation no longer served as an adequate commercial control. Delamain decided at the time to devote one of its *chais* to the aging of vintages that had been bought immediately after distillation. The company does not have direct access to this warehouse, which is now under the authority of the service for the prevention of fraud. Administration of the *chai* and maintenance of the casks is done under the auspices of this organization, which requires a carefully detailed account following each visit. Since 1989, a new amendment has permitted the sale of vintage cognacs which have been officially authenticated. This, fortunately, is the case for Delamain. Today, a vintage 1960 is on sale. It comes from a distiller in the commune of Verrières, near Segonzac.

Desmaurin

MERCHANT
CHEZ RICHON-SEGONZAC (CHARENTE)

This house of cognac is directed by Patrick Brillet, a descendant of a family of wine-growers and distillers with origins dating to 1684.

Desmaurin, located in the heart of the Grande Champagne area, specializes in cognacs made from the local grape. On offer is a Napoleon, aged ten years; an XO, aged eighteen years; and the Très Rare, aged thirty-five years.

The house also produces cognac made from the Petite Champagne grape, such as the Premier Consul, aged eight years; a Napoleon, aged ten years; and an XO, aged eighteen years. The cognacs of Desmaurin are sold in long thin bottles that are hand-blown. They are packaged in a boarded case or in a varnished wooden box. On the latter, a personalized copper plaque is featured.

Château Desmaurin, at Segonzac.

Didonne

MERCHANT
SÉMUSSAC (CHARENTE-MARITIME)
1984

Prince de Didonne is the commercial brand name of the cognac made by the winegrowing cooperative of Cozes-Saujon, located along the Gironde estuary. The cooperative includes some 150 winegrowers on about 1,235 acres in the Bons Bois area. The cooperative has its own distillery employing sixteen stills containing 660 gallons each, along with a storage capacity of 1.1 million gallons. Relatively recent in the cognac trade, the Didonne distribution company sells more than eight percent of its production on the French market, two-thirds of which are put into mass distribution, an unusual practice in today's cognac trade. The company sells numerous pineaux and wines from the Charente region, as well as five cognacs under the Prince de Didonne name. These include a Trois Étoiles, VSOP, aged six years; a Napoleon, aged nine years; an XO, aged fifteen years; and an Extra, aged twenty years. Total sales reach 850,000 bottles yearly.

Dor

MERCHANT
JARNAC (CHARENTE)
1858

Many cognac houses have disappeared over the centuries, victims of competition, buyouts, and the demise of the founding families. It is unusual in the history of cognac for a defunct house to be resurrected. Such is the case of the house of A.E. Dor. This house was originally founded by a very old Charente family who owned vineyards in Balzac and Ruffec. The company was started in 1858 in Jarnac by Amédée-Édouard Dor. His passion was for cognacs of Grande Champagne origin, which he collected and stocked in his *chais*. They were first stocked in oak casks and later transferred to demijohns that were carefully sealed with wax. His son-in-law and successor, Noël Denieul-Dor, scrupulously attended to the precious stocks. In 1972, Dor became the property of the Benedictine group which, astonishingly, showed little interest in the family passion.

PRECIOUS RESERVES

At the beginning of the 1980s, the Benedictine group was revived by a certain Jacques Rivière. His previous business experience had been in textiles, but his connections with Charente were very real indeed. His family, originally from Angeac, is known for its pineau François I, one of the first pineaus to be bottled and commercialized between the two world wars.

Jacques Rivière's decision to go into the cognac trade with his brother was in response to the desire of his wife, Odile, to have a professional activity while her husband was on the road. That decision proved to be doubly fortuitous. First, the house of Dor was in possession of some true marvels that had been forgotten, including a number of rare cognacs dating to the time before phylloxera.

Secondly, Odile Rivière developed a keen interest in cognac. Originally from Jonzac, Odile began studying cognac and cognac tasting. She contacted many cellar masters and learned everything about the art of distillation and aging. In a few short years, she became an authority on cognac,

The house of Dor owns some of the oldest vintage cognacs.

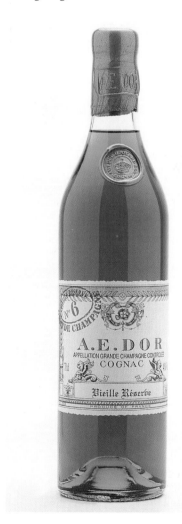

and naturally she recognized the gold mine that Benedictine had overlooked. She immediately launched a new line of cognac. But in 1992, Odile Rivière was killed in a car accident in Charente. In her memory and in honor of her almost miraculous resurrection of the name of Dor, Jacques Rivière and his children vowed to continue Odile's work, which had put Dor back on the great tables of French gastronomy.

The house of Dor became the talk of the cognac trade, largely due to its release

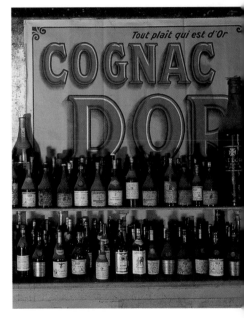

A few samples of brandy at the house of Dor, before blending.

onto the market of its oldest cognacs, such as the vintage Très Vieilles Grandes Champagnes. It also grabbed attention by obtaining the extraordinary authorization to sell its cognacs at their natural alcohol levels, which is less than forty percent by volume. The cognacs are perfectly preserved in sealed glass demijohns, which are treasures of the cognac trade and virtually inaccessible to cognac lovers. The price of these cognacs is exorbitant, thereby ensuring the preservation of the stocks for years to come. Nevertheless, the notoriety surrounding their existence has earned Dor quite a bit of good publicity.

A Charente distillery.

The Dor line includes the 1805, the oldest cognac, with an alcohol content of 30%; the Rois de Rome, from 1811, 31% alcohol by volume; and the Prince Albert, from 1834, also 30%. Next are the numbered cognacs: No. 5 (Louis-Philippe) from 1840 and 34% alcohol by volume; No. 4 (Napoleon III Empereur) from 1858, when Dor was founded, with 36% alcohol by volume; No. 3 (Prince Imperial) from 1875, 36% by volume; No. 2 (Excellence) from 1889 at 35%; and No. 1 (Age d'Or) from 1893 at 36%.

Another treasure is the line of stupendous Vieilles Réserves, which reflect the diversity of the Charente genius:

• No. 6, aged 35 years, very spicy but subtle and round.

• No. 7, aged 40 years, a strong cognac initially aggressive but smooth after lingering on the palate.

• No. 8, aged 45 years, superbly fresh and floral despite an alcohol content of 47%.

• No. 9, 1914 vintage. An exceptional blend, created by Noël Denieul, uniting 80% Grande Champagne with 20% Fins Bois. This cognac was aged for 50 years, then transferred to glass demi-johns. Renowned for its unique qualities.

• No. 11, a complex blend of old cognacs (70 years or older) that has maintained its strength at 43% alcohol by volume. This line has made the reputation of the house of A.E. Dor, since it attests to a rare expertise in the selection and blending of old cognacs. This expertise has also made for a more affordable line of cognacs, which serve as an excellent introduction to the Dor style, ranging from floral and fresh to those having stronger and more full-bodied structure.

The house also offers the Vieille Fine Champagne XO, the Napoleon (a blend of four of the best cognacs), the Rare Fine Champagne and the Selection, all made from the Fins Bois grapes and bottled in the traditional cognac styles. Two carafes are also available, the Prestige and the XO.

Drouet et Fils

MERCHANT
SALLES-D'ANGLES (CHARENTE)
1968

This family of winegrowers, established in 1915, today has some fifty-seven acres in the Grande Champagne area. They began distilling in 1968, principally for sale to the trade. In 1987, Patrick Drouet and his wife, Stéphanie (the fourth generation), decided to sell their products themselves, beginning with their pineaux des Charentes. A *chai* for aging the brandy, a bottling unit, and a tasting cellar were built. The line now includes a Trois Étoiles, aged five years; a VSOP, aged ten years; and the Réserve de Jean, aged fifteen years, named for an ancestor who won a gold medal for cognac at Brussels in 1897. Finally, Famille, aged twenty-five years, with twenty-five percent alcohol.

Duboigalant

WINEGROWER-DISTILLER-MERCHANT
SAINT-MARTIAL-SUR-NÉ
(CHARENTE-MARITIME)

Belonging to a family from Trijol that has been growing and distilling wine for generations in Charente, the brand Duboigalant includes several different cognacs made from grapes from diverse vineyards: the VSOP Fine Champagne, the XO Fine Champagne, the Borderies Très Rare (rarely commercialized for the simple reason that the vineyard yielding the grapes is so small), and the Grande Champagne Très Rare. The ages of these last two cognacs are unspecified.

Dudognon

WINEGROWER-DISTILLER-MERCHANT
LIGNIÈRES-SONNEVILLE (CHARENTE)
1776

This family has been established in the Grande Champagne area for more than two centuries. The estate comprises seventy-nine acres. Under the management of Raymond Dudognon, with the assistance of his three daughters and their husbands, the estate includes a distillery and *chais* for vinification and aging. These cognacs express the quintessential qualities of the Grand Champagne grape. Many a connoisseur considers Dudognon a favorite house.

The line begins with a VSOP, followed by a Napoleon, then the Réserve des Ancêtres, which received a gold medal in 1990, and finally the Extra Vieux.

Dumont established its *chais* on a small farm near Jarnac.

Pascal Dumont

MERCHANT
JARNAC (CHARENTE)
1987

Pascal Dumont is the grandson of a winegrower and distiller of cognac. He launched his company in 1987, in Jarnac, his home town. He set up shop at the old farm known as Bout des Ponts, whose Charente-style porch has been adopted as the company logo. In addition to his activity in wholesale, Pascal Dumont offers a selection of fine cognacs from his personal *chai* Jaune d'Or. These cognacs have diverse origins: brandies from the beginning of the century which include an XO of Fine Champagne and Grand Champagne origins, Napoleon, VSOP, and Fine Cognac. They are sold in traditional cognac bottles and also in superb carafes made of Limoges porcelain. An impressive collection of appealing spirit bottles should also be mentioned.

Dunhill

COMMERCIAL BRAND
**LA ROCHELLE
(CHARENTE-MARITIME)**

Cognac and tobacco, especially in the form of a cigar, make an excellent combination. The tobacco company Dunhill has pushed this pleasure to the point of manufacturing its own cognacs. Belonging to the tobacco concern Rothmans International, Dunhill sells just about every kind of tobacco-related product and more, including pens and watches.

Regarding its cognac venture, Dunhill turned to the house of Camus in 1995 to launch its own line, which includes above all a VSOP and an XO.

These cognacs are for the most part intended for export. They are found largely in luxury stores and in duty-free shops in airports around the world.

Dupuy

MERCHANT
COGNAC (CHARENTE)
1852

This company, devoted to selling cognac, was founded in 1852 by Auguste Dupuy. Edmond Dupuy succeeded him in 1895. In 1905, two Norwegians, Peter Rustad and Thomas Bache-Gabrielsen, bought the company and continued selling the brand. After Rustad died, the Bache-Gabrielsen family inherited full directorship of the company. René succeeded his father Thomas in 1942, and his son Christian took over from him in 1968. René Bache-Gabrielsen died in 1990, after running the company for nearly fifty years. Christian is today the director of this independent family business. He is assisted by Jean-

Philippe Bergier. The company exports ninety-four percent of its total production, or 700,000 bottles in 1995 alone. The principal markets targeted by Dupuy are Asian, especially Japan and Taiwan, and Norway, Canada, Belgium, and Germany.

At Dupuy, in 1900.

The Dupuy line of cognacs is vast, extending from a Trois Étoiles to the Grande Fine Champagne Hors d'Âge. The bottles vary considerably themselves as far as style is concerned. A different style is used for each market. Dupuy also has a license that allows it to produce cognacs for the perfume company Rochas.

EF

Exshaw

John Exshaw was descended from an old Irish family. One of his relatives was once Lord Mayor of Dublin. Like many of his compatriots at the time, he came to Bordeaux, in 1802, and three years later entered the wine and spirits trade. It was the habit of the British back then to purchase very young brandies and to let

Of Irish origin, John Exshaw created his brandy trade in 1805.

them age along the docks of London. John Exshaw differed with this practice and was of the opinion that the climate of southwest France was more favorable to the aging of cognac. He therefore

decided to age the brandy himself before exporting it to Great Britain. Due to this practice, his cognacs achieved an outstanding reputation. To bypass the blockade in effect during the Napoleonic wars, Exshaw employed ships flying the American flag to export, or smuggle, his cognac to Britain. He was also one of the first to show interest in the markets of the Far East. He was obliged, however, to transport his cognac overland by camel since at that time the Suez Canal had not yet been built. His eldest son, Thomas-Henri, continued in his father's footsteps and used the far-flung British Empire as a means of commercializing his cognac throughout the Orient, from Mauritius to the Indies. The decline of the British Empire following the World War II resulted in substantial losses to the business, which had focused its activity mainly on Northern Europe and the Far East while specializing in high-quality cognacs.

In 1975, Exshaw was finally bought out by Otard, which has itself since become the property of the Bacardi-Martini group. The company essentially sells the XO No. 1, made exclusively of brandies of Grande Champagne origin, aged fifteen to twenty years; and the Extra Âge d'Or, also of Grande Champagne origin and aged twenty-five years.

Falandy

MERCHANT
COGNAC (CHARENTE)
1974

This company has essentially devoted all of its efforts to the Southeast Asian markets of China and Hong Kong. The cognacs, sold under the names Falandy and Liandry, are bottled in a *chai* in Cognac. The line includes a VSOP, a Napoleon, an XO and the Très Vieille Réserve.

In Grande Champagne, the chalk is sometimes visible at ground level.

Pierre Ferrand

DISTILLER-MERCHANT
CHÂTEAU DE BONBONNET-ARS (CHARENTE)
1992

It was in 1986 that two business school students, Alexandre Gabriel and Jean-Dominique Andreu, went looking for a traditional type of business to which they could apply modern management methods as a school project. They found their opportunity in the person of Pierre Ferrand, a winegrower and distiller from La Nérolle in the heart of the Grande Champagne area. Pierre Ferrand was in possession of some high-quality stocks of cognac, but sales were not up to par.

In 1992, the two students and Pierre Ferrand became partners. The two students got eight percent of the stake in the Pierre Ferrand brand name and products, with the rest going to Pierre Ferrand himself. Alexandre Gabriel was hardly an amateur in the winegrowing and distilling business, having come from a family of growers and distillers in Burgundy. Together, their knowhow paid off handsomely, and sales of Pierre Ferrand began to take off, especially in the United States and the Far East.

However, relations between the partners rapidly deteriorated. Gabriel and Andreu were unhappy with the quality of cognac that Pierre Ferrand was producing; he felt they were exploiting his name and his labor. No official breakup of the partnership occurred, but the two camps went their separate ways. Gabriel and Andreu sought out other suppliers and purchased the *chais* of the château de Bonbonnet, which belonged to Martell at the time. They developed their own line of cognacs from that point on. Pierre Ferrand attempted to reclaim the use of his own name. He finally went into partnership with another producer, Franck G. Monier, from Chassors near Jarnac in the Fins Bois area (see Monier-Ferrand).

Despite their youth and inexperience, the young Turks had a clear idea of what a top-of-the-line cognac should be. They were convinced that finding the right combination of elements for making a cognac was the best way for a new business to establish itself in such a competitive market. Their innovation was to distill the wine with the dregs, instead of removing the dregs before each operation. They also preferred using small stills and immediate distillation as soon as the wine had fermented. Reduction of the alcohol is carefully performed by the addition of small amounts of water over an extended period. Humidity is also scrupulously controlled with the use of water sprays. The cognac is aged in "red" casks of Limousin oak and the bottles are meticulously rinsed with cognac prior to being filled.

Panoramic view of the vineyards of Grande Champagne.

Only cognacs of Grande Champagne origin are sold under the name of Pierre Ferrand. They include the Ambre, aged 8 to 12 years; the Réserve, aged 20 to 30 years; the Sélection des Anges, aged 30 to 40 years and identified by production lot; the Ancestrale, 70 years old or older; and finally, a limited production of 200 to 300 bottles a year that are custom-made and bottled. The blends are always made of cognacs of the same origins and no colorants or additives are allowed.

Under the brand name of Gabriel & Andreu, an original line of four cognacs is offered, each of a different origin with unique qualities. They include the Fins Bois, aged 8 years and 40% alcohol by volume, from Jarnac; the Borderies, aged 15 years and 40% by volume from the region of Saint-André; the Petite Champagne, aged 25 years and 42% by volume, from Archiac; and finally the Grande Champagne, aged 35 years and 43% by volume, from Segonzac. Each numbered bottle bears the lot number to which it belongs and the bottling date.

Lastly, the company features a line of cognacs destined for the Asian market and sold under the brand name of Landy. They are sold in a carafe which is a replica in glass of an old-time ship, an intricately crafted object that clearly required the efforts of an artisan. Twelve different models were produced, followed by another set representing the 12 signs of the Chinese zodiac.

Jean Fillioux

MERCHANT
JUILLAC-LE-COQ (CHARENTE)
1880

The estate of La Pouyade, in the heart of Grande Champagne.

In 1880, Honoré Fillioux established a vineyard and cognac business on the domain of La Pouyade in Juillac-le-Coq in the heart of the Grande Champagne area. His son, Jean Fillioux, later presided over the family business, and it is under his name that the cognac is sold today. His son Michel would in turn succeed him. Today, Pascal Fillioux, of the fourth generation, is in charge of the company. The name Fillioux belongs to a famous line of cellar masters who were responsible for quality control at the Hennessy works. Nevertheless, the family was in the first place makers of cognac of Grande Champagne origin. They favor a distillation in the presence of the dregs, use of a *brouillis* of less than thirty percent alcohol, and a *bonne chauffe* exceeding seventy percent alcohol. "If by this approach we obtain a more aggressive brandy to start with, then in the long run there will be a more developed bouquet, flavor, and texture after the aging process is complete," Pascal Fillioux explains. The aging is done in casks made exclusively of oak from Limousin.

The line includes the Coq, aged 3 to 4 years; the Pouyade, aged 7 to 8 years and the only cognac containing 42% alcohol by volume; the Napoleon, aged 8 to 9 years; the Cep d'Or, aged 12 to 13 years; and the Réserve Familiale in a carafe, aged more than 45 years.

Forgeron

WINEGROWER-DISTILLER-MERCHANT
SEGONZAC (CHARENTE)
1965

Bought on the cheap in 1902, shortly after the phylloxera crisis, by the grandfather of Michel Forgeron, the vineyards have been exploited for the last two generations by mixed farming. The farm is located at "Chez Richon" in Segonzac. In 1960, Michel Forgeron inherited the farm, which included five acres of vineyards and ten acres of farmland, along with the facilities needed for making cognac. A horse was also thrown into the bargain. He began by regrouping the lands and alternating the crops, but later decided to develop the vineyards to better exploit the land of the Grande Champagne. Following his marriage in 1965 to Francine, he purchased a still and began distilling cognac. In 1977, they began selling their cognacs, relying largely on word of mouth to promote their products. Today, the operation includes forty acres of vineyards, a physical plant for producing cognac, and a sizable production stock. The son of Michel and Francine Forgeron is being groomed to succeed them.

The line includes a Trois Étoiles, a VSOP (11 years, 43% alcohol by volume); the Vieille Réserve (18 years; 45%); and the Hors d'Âge Special (26 years; 50%). The latter is uncut and unblended. Also on offer are two pineaux.

Frapin

WINEGROWER-DISTILLER-MERCHANT
SEGONZAC (CHARENTE)
MIDDLE OF NINETEENTH CENTURY

This large company owns the largest vineyard in Grande Champagne, and all of its cognacs are made exclusively from Grande Champagne grapes—a rare example of its kind in the world of cognac. The Frapin family is an old Charente family and its lineage can be traced back to 1270. A number of the ancestors are famous. For example, François Rabelais was the consequence of one of Catherine Frapin's frolics. In the next century, Pierre Frapin was Louis XIV's apothecary and the family's heraldry is due to him.

As the family proliferated, it was another Pierre Frapin who, at the end of the last century, turned to the commercialization of the family's cognac production. Frapin, who was also mayor of Segonzac for more than twenty years, won numerous awards for the impeccable quality of his cognacs, including gold medals at the World Expositions in Paris in 1889 and 1900. Other awards came from the countries to which he exported his cognac. In 1898, Félix Faure, then president of the Republic, praised the good work being done by the Frapin family, whose Grande Champagne vineyards were considered to be the best tended in the area.

One of Pierre Frapin's daughters went on to marry André Renaud, the man who succeeded in lifting Rémy Martin to the highest rungs of the cognac trade. The connections between the two families grew even closer when another daughter, Geneviève, married Max Cointreau. For thirty-six years, Max was the CEO of that celebrated house of liqueurs from Angers. He was not, however, the major stockholder of Rémy Martin and so was unable to gain control of the company despite years of legal battles. He therefore decided to focus his attention on the Frapin holdings. Already an expert in cognac (he distilled his first *bonne chauffe* in 1942 with André Renaud in Juilliac-le-Coq), Max developed exports while instructing his daughter, Béatrice, on the ins and outs of the cognac trade. She eventually joined him at the head of the company, which is presided over today by Geneviève Cointreau. Béatrice was one of the youngest of Max's seven children and the only one who had any real interest in the family business. Following her law, business, and marketing studies in the United States, Béatrice devoted herself to working in advertising before finally returning to the cognac trade in the mid-1980s. Today, she also directs the champagne company Gosset, which was acquired in 1994. In terms of distribution, especially in the area of exports, these two family-style businesses have helped to significantly boost each other's sales.

The Frapin vineyard, 494 acres situated in the best area, the Grande Champagne.

TRADITION AND MODERNITY

The average size of a vineyard in the Grande Champagne area is thirty acres. The vineyards of Frapin, in contrast, cover 740 acres, 494 of which are used just for growing the vines, which are of the ugni blanc variety. The distillery and the different *chais* used for aging the cognac are located on the premises or nearby in the town of Segonzac, where the company's headquarters are situated. This formidable establishment allows Frapin to directly control the whole production line right in the middle of the best land used for growing the grapes.

Frapin has also amassed a large stock of some of the highest-quality cognacs. The whole operation relies on the use of both traditional techniques and those more recently developed. Modern methods, however, are only employed when they make for a noticable improvement in the quality of the cognac. The vines themselves are fertilized with cow manure and mulch obtained from the winter trimming of the vines. The latter accounts for fifty percent of the plant's organic needs. At the end of the winter, what remains of the wine following distillation is also added to the soil. This system assures the efficient use of every aspect of the vine and cuts down on costs.

Frapin has recently invested in four new wine presses which preserve the quality of the grapes. These presses are put to use within a few hours of the harvest and allow for a more careful and controlled dripping of the juices from the grapes, which adds to the freshness and bouquet of the wines.

The distillation of the unfiltered wine takes place in four stills, each with a volume of 660 gallons. The initial aging of the brandy occurs over a year in casks newly made from Limousin oak. The cognac is then transferred to older casks in which the aging process will be completed. Various *chais* with different temperatures and degrees of humidity are used by the quality control expert, Olivier Paultes, to obtain a more harmonious aging. The casks are regularly rotated between these different warehouses, depending on the brandy's stage of development. Recently, a fire protection system has been installed in all of the *chais*.

The line of cognacs offered by Frapin has recently been refocused to emphasize the higher quality categories, all of which are of Grande Champagne origin. These cognacs are notable for their fine aromatic qualities, effect on the palate, and delicious aftertaste:

• VSOP, aged 8 years on average, is the only VSOP cognac on the market of exclusively Grande Champagne origin.

• The VIP XO is sold in a carafe, inspired by a sixteenth-century flagon, which has gold trimming around the bottom and a gold plated cap.

• The Extra, Réserve Patrimonial Pierre Frapin, is sold in a crystal carafe.

• The Château Fontpinot, named after the family properties, is a Frapin exclusive. It is made from a single growth on a vineyard of 358 acres. The grapes are picked, the wine distilled, the brandy aged, and the cognac bottled all on the premises.

• The Domaine Frapin, aged 15 to 20 years, is a woodier tasting cognac due to the use of entirely new oak casks for the aging process.

• The Baccarat Rabelais was created for the five hundredth birthday of the bard. This cognac is exceptionally fine on the palate with a remarkable aftertaste. It is a blend of some of the estate's oldest reserves. Some of the brandies date to before the phylloxera blight. The carafe is inspired by a sixteenth-century flagon and is decorated with gold-plated effigies of Renaissance symbols: the peacock, the Book of Knowledge, and the Horns of Abundance. It should be noted that this carafe is the successor of another made from Baccarat crystal and sold by Frapin. The beveled carafe is decorated by an eagle on the cap and can still be found in some stores. The cognacs of Frapin have enjoyed a remarkable popularity in recent years and sales have been growing faster than the market itself. These cognacs are for the most part intended for export, notably to Taiwan and Germany.

Fussigny

MERCHANT
JARNAC (CHARENTE)
1988

Louis Royer, the house of cognac founded in the last century in Jarnac, was sold in 1988 to the Japanese conglomerate Suntory, much to the displeasure of Alain-Louis Royer, who otherwise would have inherited it. His origins in Charente date to the eighteenth century; he descended from a long line of winegrowers, coopers, distillers, and cognac merchants. Following the loss of Louis Royer, he was determined to establish his own. He was well-equipped to go into the business, having a solid background in marketing and management as well as extensive contacts throughout the world, in particular with the United States. The house was dubbed A. de Fussigny, after one of his wife's ancestors. Her maiden name was Anne-Marie Pantin de Fussigny and her ancestor was a renowned winegrower, agronomist, and adventurer.

A UNIQUE COLLECTION

Alain Royer began his business by traveling around Charente in search of fine cognacs. He knew the region well and had many friends there. His wife also helped him select the cognacs they intended to commercialize. His idea was to buy cognac from the distillers and smaller producers who, having sold the bulk of their production to the larger houses, normally retained a small portion for their own consumption. Little by little, he acquired a unique collection of cognacs, which soon drew the attention of cognac authorities the world over and earned him a reputation as one of the foremost purveyors of fine cognac. Several famous restaurants, including Lucas Carton and the Auberge de l'Ill, offer the Fussigny cognacs. In contrast to the practice of many in his profession, Alain Royer is more than willing to supply his clients with any information about the nature and origins of his cognacs. Fussigny has also innovated with respect to the bottling of its cognacs. The bottles are made of clear glass and shaped in the famous old style of the tall flagon that was hand-blown in Bordeaux. Slightly asymmetric, the neck of the bottle is somewhat off center and the bottle itself is sealed with a cap made of cork and wood.

The labels are also very original. They are the result of an encounter between Alain-Louis Royer and a Bordeaux painter named Michel Bardin. In a modernist style, Michel Bardin has managed to capture the ambiance of the different areas around Charente, its countryside and vineyards. As many of the smaller houses of cognac were failing or being bought out, the appearance of Fussigny and its almost astonishing success on the international scene can only stand as a testimony to the merchants of Charente and their indisputable genius for cognac.

This line of cognacs favors more floral qualities and shows a clear disdain for the woodier varieties. The line begins with an XO, which reflects the uncompromising devotion to cognac found at Fussigny. Called Lot 099, it is made from a blend comprising 60% Petite Champagne, from Archiac for the most part but also from Saint-Amant and Angeac; 30% Fins Bois from Métairies and Foussignac; and 10% Grande Champagne from Saint-Preuil. The blend is further aged in oak casks to harmonize the different characteristics of each cognac.

Even rarer is the Heritage Lot 102, a well-rounded and subtle blend involving Petite Champagne from Archiac (70%), and two Grandes Champagnes from Lignières and Segonzac.

The Fine Champagne Vieille Réserve is the result of a blend involving 60% Grande Champagne from Lignières, aged 30 years, and 40% Petite Champagne from Sainte-Lheurine, near Archiac, aged 20 years. The alcohol content in the blend is reduced by the addition of old cognacs diluted to 15% alcohol by volume using distilled water.

The Très Vieille Grande Champagne is an exceptional lot coming from Bonneuil. The aging of this cognac in oak casks exceeds 50 years and has a natural unreduced alcohol content of 42% by volume.

These last two lots are of limited quantity and are stamped as such. When these stocks are exhausted, other lots will be sold in their place. Let the cognac fan be notified.

Gautier

WINEGROWER-DISTILLER-MERCHANT
AIGRE (CHARENTE)
1755

Although confined to the outer limits in the north of the Charente, Aigre played an early and important role in the cognac trade. Its location on the old royal road from Paris passing through Orléans and Châtellerault had the advantage that the tolls exacted on goods were significantly less if they were sent overland through Aigre than if sent by river or sea. In 1804, there were four brandy merchants in Aigre compared to six in Cognac itself. They were all bought out by Gautier over time. The oldest existing document by which the company can be dated goes back to 1755, but it is likely that the company is considerably older than that. The Gautier family came from Cher and moved to Aigre in the seventeenth century following the marriage of Charles Gautier to a certain Jacquette Brochet. Charles owned some vineyards and it is probable that his grandson Louis (1678-1733), sieur de La Plaine, was the first member of the family to begin selling cognac. The family was to remain active in business over several generations until the death of Joseph in 1913. His nephew, Michel Hériard-Dubreuil, who had married Simone,

Inside a *chai* used for aging cognac. The aging of the brandy is not just a matter of waiting. The casks are frequently moved in order to regulate and vary humidity and temperature, which is indispensable for obtaining a fine cognac.

the daughter of Joseph, assumed control of the company until 1942 and was in turn succeeded by his son Gonzague. In 1970, the company was bought by the Berger group which expanded sales of the cognac, especially on the French market. In 1995, Berger itself merged with the Bordeaux group Marie-Brizard.

The location of the *chais* used for aging the cognacs is unique: They were built on a little island in the middle of a small river, a location that guarantees an optimal range of humidity. Most of the installations date back to 1880. At one time, the house owned vineyards, but today all of its efforts are concentrated on sales.

The Gautier line extends from a Trois Étoiles to the XO Gold and the Extra Crystal. Gautier was one of the first houses to design and use packaging that was meant to appeal to Asian consumers, who like to collect the more fancifully designed bottles. Among the more curious designs that have been used are fisherman's floats tied together with rope, lanterns, and even a tiller containing a flask of cognac. Gautier has also commercialized different flagons made of porcelain in the shape of the Concorde (in white, midnight blue, and even gold-plated), and another frivolity shaped like the Sydney opera house. Recently, Gautier has introduced the Tradition Rare Dixième Génération, a blend of old cognacs that have been conserved for a long time in their *paradis*. Production is limited to 2,400 numbered bottles. The company Gemaco, which sells brandies and the Normandin and Pascal Combeau cognacs, is part of the same group and is also located at Aigre.

Jules Gautret

MERCHANT

JONZAC (CHARENTE-MARITIME)

1847

The distiller and merchant Jules Gautret began operating in the middle of the last century and eventually developed a trade network throughout France and Europe. In 1959, the company merged with a newly created cooperative of winegrowers called Unicognac, based in Jonzac. Unicognac has never stopped growing and today it represents some 2,500 winegrowers and a variety of different cognacs. Unicognac also owns its own distillery employing sixteen stills each with a capacity of 660 gallons. The aging is done in fourteen different *chais*. The group sells about 300,000 cases of cognac and pineau des Charente each year.

The Jules Gautret line includes a Trois Étoiles, a VSOP, a Napoleon, an XO, and an Extra. Also on offer are three different pineaux des Charentes, including an Extra Vieux sold in a carafe. But Unicognac itself sells a number of different cognacs, some of which are made for a particular export market:

• Ansac, launched a dozen years ago, is intended for the American market.

• Roi des Rois is sold only in duty-free shops. These cognacs are mainly sold in carafes, but they also come in different porcelain flagons.

Godet

MERCHANT
**LA ROCHELLE
(CHARENTE-MARITIME)**
1838

In the late sixteenth century, a Dutch merchant named Bonaventure Godet settled near the town of Marennes in the Charente-Maritime. His initial interest was in exporting salt from the local marshes, but he also traded in wine. His name looks like a typical French name, but it comes in fact from the Dutch word *codde*, which refers to a cylindrical piece of wood. In French it signifies a small drinking glass. The Godet family enjoyed an almost immediate success in France, and in 1588, Henri IV authorized them to carry an *épée* (sword) as a sign of their status as merchants. In 1730, Augustin Godet moved to La Rochelle and began doing business

Inside the distillery at Godet.

with England and other Northern European countries. It wasn't until 1838, however, that the descendants of Augustin turned to the selling of cognac under their own name. At the time, Gédéon Godet Jr. developed a special blend of cognacs, the Gastronome, which still exists today, even though its recipe (a guarded secret) was altered somewhat in 1920. Jean Godet was to put his mark on the family business when he took control in 1920. President until 1970, he left for the United States and lived there some twelve years while overseeing distribution of the family cognac on the American market. The effort in America paid off handsomely and the success there was surprising given the small-family style of the business. Their motto suits them well: "We choose our cognacs like we choose our friends."

Since 1984, the company has been managed by Jean-Jacques Godet with the assistance of his brother Jean-Marie. The company produces over one million bottles a year and maintains a stock ten times that size in its warehouses (covering 2.5 acres) at La Rochelle.

The line includes:

- The Cuvée Jean Godet (Fins Bois, Borderies and Bons Bois), considered to be superior in quality to a VS.
- The Sélection Spéciale (Bons Bois, Fins Bois), aged between 6 and 8 years.
- The Gastronome, VSOP Fine Champagne, which includes at least 8 cognacs of Grande Champagne origin.
- The Napoleon (Fins Bois, Borderies and Bons Bois and aged 15 years), is sold in a glass flagon and bears the image of a bust of the Emperor.
- The Excellence (Grandes and Petites Champagnes and Borderies, aged 25 years).
- The XO Fine Champagne, aged 30 years and sold in a carafe.
- The Grande Champagne, aged 50 years and sold in a Saint-Louis carafe.

- The Renaissance, a Grande Champagne also sold in a carafe.

The new packaging used for the Excellence and the Sélection Spéciale should also be noted. They are sold together in two square bottles of 50 centiliters each, which is more practical for people who are traveling. There is also available a flagon shaped like a ship's anchor and made of Limoges porcelain. Godet also produces a number of pineaux aged 10 years (red and white).

A portrait of Louis Godet about 1900.

Léopold Gourmel

MERCHANT
GENTÉ (CHARENTE)
1979

Pierre Voisin, an engineer, was originally from Cognac. Toward the end of the 1950s, he began to accumulate a nice collection of cognacs. He then bought his first casks in order to better understand the aging process. After twenty years of research, he started his own company in 1979 with the help of his daughter, named for her grandfather, Léopold Gourmel. A horse's head is the company logo, and it is a reminder that Léopold was a saddle maker on the Ile de Ré.

The house of Léopold Gourmel made something of a sensation with its partic-ularly aromatic blends, its own personal classification of cognac, and its innovative packaging techniques.

By emphasizing that cognac is above all a wine-based brandy, Pierre Voisin was careful to choose the plots on which the grapes are grown. He created his line of cognacs of Fins Bois origin from grapes grown in two different areas: the hillsides of Tarsac and Moulidars. He also uses grapes from Petite Champagne (Archiac).

The wine is ten percent alcohol by volume as opposed to the usual eight or nine percent. It is distilled with the dregs. The resulting brandy is sixty-eight percent alcohol by volume, which is slightly below the average. The brandy is then aged in casks made of oak from the banks of the Loire. The new casks are used only for the first eight to nine months of aging, and the brandy is then transferred to older "red" casks to complete the process. The alcohol is carefully reduced by adding distilled water over a period from thirty-six months to seven years, depending on the quality of the cognac.

The blends never employ cognacs made from grapes coming from different vineyards or harvests. Neither syrup, caramel, or any flavor-enhancing additives are used. The cognacs are never refrigerated nor filtered at low temperature and they are bottled after the flagons are rinsed.

These intricate procedures may be expensive but the result is clear: these cognacs are significantly different from most of the cognacs produced in Charente. They tend to be paler in color but their aromas are of a much more subtle quality and their overall flavors are well defined.

Contrary to the standard classification of cognacs, Pierre Voisin has divided his goods into four poetic categories, which characterize the special qualities of each cognac, from the youngest to the oldest. These include the Âge de fruit, Âge des fleurs, Âge des épices and Quintessence, respectively. These denominations also account for the aromas that dominate each stage of the aging process. The cognacs are sold in tall bottles and carafes, bulbous in shape for the Âge des fruits and the Âge des fleurs, or conical for the Âge des epices and the Quintessence.

The outstanding quality of the Gourmel cognacs has earned praise from restaurateurs and connoisseurs as well as numerous other cognac experts. It is all the more remarkable that these cognacs are largely of Fins Bois origin, which usually makes for a lower quality cognac. About sixty percent of the production is exported and the company maintains stocks representing some fifteen years worth of production.

H

Hardy

MERCHANT
COGNAC (CHARENTE)
1863

Antoine Hardy was a cognac merchant of British origin. He moved to Charente to develop his links to the cognac trade as a middleman, and three years later, he adopted French nationality and went into the business of selling his own cognacs. With a natural flair for business, Hardy took advantage of the free-trade agreement Napoleon III had signed with Great Britain and immediately engaged in intense trade activity with his former homeland. Toward the end of the century, rising taxes made trade with Britain difficult, so Hardy turned to the vast Russian market. This was the golden age of trade between Russia and France.

His son and descendants continued the business, which remains today a family affair. Since 1945, the company has been under the direction of Jacques, Hardy's

Antoine Hardy, the company's founder.

A typical cognac house on the banks of the Charente River.

81

great-grandson, along with other members of the family. For example, Jacques' daughters, Bénédicte and Sophie, are in charge of marketing and public relations, respectively. Only Francis, Jacques' brother, opted for the world of politics, and has served as mayor and representative from Cognac.

Having initially specialized in wholesale, the house of Hardy has for the past forty years commercialized its own brand of cognac, with the rooster as a mascot. The house also became the talk of the cognac world when, in the 1980s, it sold one of the oldest in existence, a Grande Champagne dating back to before the phylloxera blight. Only 1,200 bottles were put up for sale in carafes made of crystal by Daum. Each carafe was accompanied by a certificate guaranteeing its authenticity and a reproduction of a painting by Carzou specially made for the occasion. In 1990, an importer from Chicago sold the last thirty-six carafes from this lot, which had been dubbed Perfection. Each bottle sold for the modest price of 3,500 dollars. This whole escapade proved to be brilliant publicity for the house of Hardy.

In terms of sales, Hardy led the French market a few years ago, though largely due to cognacs made especially for mass distribution. In terms of the competition worldwide, Hardy ranks a solid tenth in sales.

Capitalizing on the penchant of many cognac lovers for a fine cigar while relaxing with a favorite cognac, Hardy began distribution of a cigar from Santo Domingo, El Sublimado. In 1991, they hit upon the

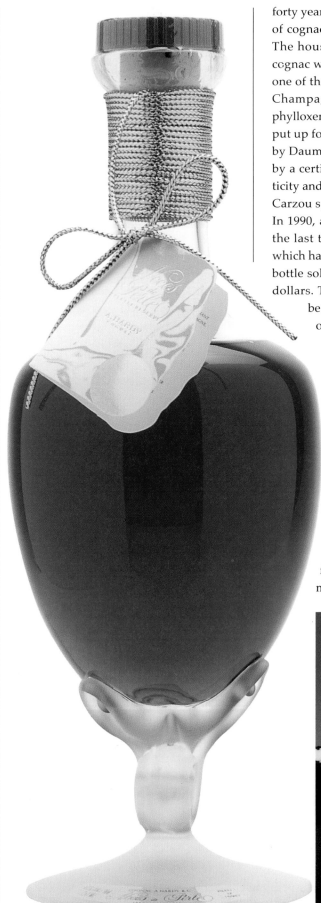

idea of developing a cigar made especially for cognac, a cigar that shared the aromatic qualities of the cognac itself. The tobacco leaves, which come from the Caribbean, are steeped in XO Hardy cognac, and then fermented six months prior to being rolled.

Credit for this innovative idea is due to Sophie Hardy, who, during a voyage through South America, witnessed smokers dunking their cigars in brandy before lighting them up. With this concept,

which is registered of course, Hardy, in effect, expanded the horizons of expectation among merchants of cognac and other spirits. Original though the idea may be, one wonders if it will really catch on with the consumer, who has been trying to kick the habit of tobacco and alcohol for years.

The Hardy line includes the VS (Fins Bois and Borderies); the VSOP Fine Champagne (aged 5 to 8 years), both of which are sold in long bottles with reinforced bases; and the XO, the standard bearer of the house, which is sold in a fancy bottle mounted on a pedestal. The more exclusive members of the line, all of Grande Champagne origin, are associated with a nuptial theme: the Noces de Diamant, sold in a carafe; the Noces de Perle (aged on average 30 years), is sold in a carafe of an Art Nouveau style, and finally the Noces d'Or (aged 50 years). A second version, sold in a special carafe called the Capitaine, won an Oscar for packaging.

Buildings of the house of Hardy.

Hennessy

WINEGROWER-DISTILLER-MERCHANT
COGNAC (CHARENTE)
1765

No matter what the legend may be behind this "brave and gallant" gentleman, little could he have realized, when he settled in Charente in 1760, that he would lay the foundations of the world's largest house of cognac. He was the youngest son of the Irish Lord Ballymacmoy. At the age of twenty-six, he enlisted in the Irish brigade of Louis XV. He was wounded at the battle of Fontenoy in 1745 and was dispatched to the Ile de Ré, where the young Irishman discovered the charms of Charente . . . and the lucrative cognac trade.

He proved to be an energetic and shrewd businessman, working first at Ostende and Dunkerque, where he was associated with a Tonnay-Charente company.

Obviously, Richard Hennessy understood quickly the far-reaching appeal of the Charente cognacs. He realized that his family connections in Ireland could be of invaluable service. He therefore started his own cognac business at Cognac in 1765 and then left for Bordeaux, leaving the operation in the hands of his partner, Saule. Upon his return in 1778, he resumed control of the business with his son Jacques.

Jacques developed the trade with the flourishing United States market. In 1792, Hennessy exported the equivalent of 240,000 cases of cognac to America. Hennessy can also claim to be the first company ever to make a sale in New York, in 1794. The descendants of the buyer, Jacob Shieffelin, are still loyal clients of the house of Hennessy some two hundred years later. Astutely, Jacques Hennessy married Marthe Henriette Martell, establishing a bond between the two families. It was also Jacques who would give the company the name it bears today: Jas Hennessy & Cie. Of his three sons, James turned out to be the most talented when it came to expanding the company's operations. In 1832, exports reached a staggering 655,000 cases. Northern Europe and North America were the main clients.

Maurice Hennessy (1834-1905), of the fourth generation, would in his turn considerably influence the expansion of the company. At that time, cognac was sold only in barrels, which made it easy to counterfeit. In 1865, the company started bottling their cognac as a means of guaranteeing its authenticity, making Hennessy one of the originators of this procedure. Maurice Hennessy also introduced the idea of dividing cognac up into different classes depending on the quality. He got the idea from his uncle Auguste

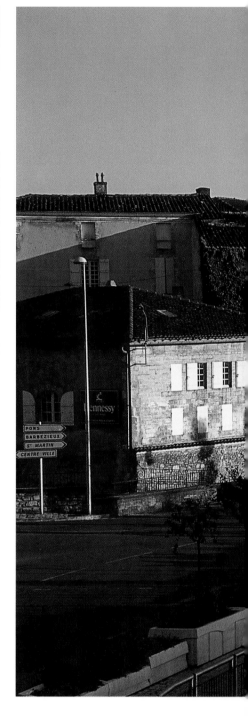

and put it into practice when, finding a star engraved on the window of an office at the works, he proposed using a different number of stars to represent each year a cognac had been aged, ranging from one to three. The Trois Étoiles was born.

Whenever a new market opens, you can be sure to find Hennessy there, be it Russia, Japan, Australia, Thailand, Mexico, etc. The "armed arm," the brand's logo, comes from the Hennessy coat of

The headquarters of Hennessy are in the heart of the historic quarter of Cognac, beside the Charente.

arms in Ireland. There was also a wild boar on the coat of arms, but it was probably dropped in the belief that it might have a potentially negative impact on sales.

Despite the upheavals of the twentieth century, Hennessy has never ceased to expand and consolidate its conquests, maintaining its position throughout the turmoil at the top of the charts. In 1984, the mark of two million cases sold was reached, and in 1991, the three million

mark was easily attained. Since the economic crises, Hennessy sales have only slightly dropped though the overall market has suffered considerably. In 1995, it claimed 28.5 percent of the market compared with 17.5 percent in 1979.

In the meantime, the structure of the company has changed significantly. In 1971, Hennessy merged with Moët & Chandon, a leading champagne company. The company's integrity has remained

intact, and it has generously benefited from the enormous distribution network now available to both partners. The agreement was finally completed in 1987, with the creation of the group LVMH (Louis Vuitton-Moët-Hennessy), which is today the number one merchant of luxury items—from fashion goods (Dior) to champagne and, of course, cognac. Things really took off when one of the world's heavyweights in the beer and alcohol trade, Guinness, joined the team.

Nevertheless, it is the descendants of Richard Hennessy who remain in control of the cognac operation. Alain de Pracomtal and then Henri de Pracomtal in 1992, are of the sixth and seventh generations, respectively, to run the show. The company's vice-president, Gilles Hennessy, is one of the leading publicists of the brand, appearing in commercials for the cognac in Germany and the Far East.

THE INFLUENCE OF A LEADER

A few figures will give an idea of just what Hennessy is about. The company possesses fifteen different vineyards, which are responsible for only a negligible part of the raw material used in

The very old cognacs in the Hennessy *paradis* **are stored in old casks or glass demijohns.**

making their cognacs. They also own twenty-seven distilleries and forty-two *chais* for aging, with a capacity of 260,000 barrels. Some 2,600 winegrowers are under contract with Hennessy. There are two cask manufacturers under Hennessy's control, of which Taransaud is the largest in the region. They manufacture 21,000 barrels each year. The wood comes from a forest of several hundred acres that is also owned by Hennessy.

If there is a Hennessy dynasty, there is also a Fillioux dynasty. Since the beginning of this century, the Fillioux family has furnished Hennessy with their cellar masters. Yann Fillioux is the seventh generation of the family to hold that esteemed position at Hennessy. Altogether, that represents some two centuries of quality control assured by the same family lines—which perhaps accounts for the consistent quality of Hennessy over the ages. Indeed, such a long affiliation between a family and a brandy suggests an underlying genetic link.

Yann Fillioux and his small ring of tasters sample twice a year the contents of each and every cask to control the aging of the cognac. They use a grid of twenty different criteria, with additional criteria for a more nuanced appraisal. Each grid is then subjected to computer analysis and the result is calculated.

Thanks to the enormous stocks maintained by the company, the cognac

earned unimaginable royalties, given that the XO has become an undisputed standard of quality, especially in Asia. The famous carafe shaped like a grape leaf dates from 1947.

• The Paradis, a concoction of Maurice Fillioux, is the true quintessence of Hennessy. It is a blend of supposedly several hundred different cognacs taken from the oldest stocks held by the house.

Maurice Fillioux, using the general title of the "search for harmony," compared the cognacs of the house of Hennessy to music: the VS was similar to a Gershwin composition for its ardor and modernity; the VSOP evoked Mozart for its ineffable charm, and the XO was quite simply Beethoven for its presence and variety.

As for the cherished Paradis, for Maurice it was as perfectly composed as French

remains consistent from year to year, whatever the variations may be with regard to the harvest and the viscissitudes of the aging process.

The cognacs on offer are, however, surprisingly restricted:

• The VS (Very Special), successor to the Trois Étoiles created by Maurice Hennessy.

• The VSOP Privilège, whose name derives from an order placed in 1817 by the Prince Regent of England, the future George IV, for a "Very Superior Old Pale." At the time, this referred not to an age of cognac but rather to a cognac that had not been colored or sweetened with caramel or molasses.

• The XO, created in 1870 by Maurice Hennessy for family and friends. If he had registered this brand, it would have

A distillery at Hennessy, and the barrel museum.

music from the nineteenth century.

The rarest cognac of the house, the No 1, is not for sale, being reserved for an exclusive elite. Most of the company executives have only tasted it once or twice. Finally, in 1995, Hennessy launched some new products on a few select markets. They are the Choice, targeting China; Privé, intended for Japan; and the Extra de Bagnolet and the Bras d'Or, distributed only on the duty-free network.

Hennessy exports ninety-nine percent of its products, but is nevertheless active in the French market. Faced with declining sales in France, however, Hennessy has been obliged to innovate new modes

of consumption. The result was the Hennessy Glace, released during the 1980s in just about every trendy bar in France. Its gimmick was the use of a special bottle with a number of musical devices in mind such as karaoke. More recently, the Hennessy Café has appeared; this is a small sample of VS or VSOP in a tiny tulip-shaped glass, served with coffee at restaurants.

PATRON OF THE ARTS

In Cognac itself, Hennessy has purchased a number of the older houses and converted them into warehouses without altering their external appearances. These are visited by hundreds of thousands of tourists each year. Recently, the Hennessy museum, situated on the banks of the Charente, was entirely redone. Reconstruction was overseen by the architect Jean-Michel Wilmotte, who combined the older buildings with a newer one of copper, wood, glass, and stone to suggest authenticity. The complete tour includes the *chais* for aging the cognac, located on the right bank of the river where the oldest brandies are kept, followed by a visit to the museum on the left bank. The tour provides a complete panoramic view of the history of the company, with additional features, such as a short film by Yves Angelo comparing the making of cognac to the composition of a symphony. The cooperage leg of the tour features an interesting collection of rare and unusual objects.

Abroad, the promotion of Hennessy exploits a multitude of cultural and artistic activities. Sponsoring musical events such as symphony or jazz concerts is frequently used by the company to keep its name in the public eye. Musical evenings in Italy, opera in Japan, recitals of Rostropovich in Asia, or amateur jazz orchestra contests in America are just a few examples of Hennessy's support for the arts.

In 1990, the Hennessy Mozart fellowship was created. It is awarded each year to a young musician for an original interpretation of a violin work by Mozart. In 1991, Hennessy commissioned two violins, a viola, and a cello from the instrument maker Jean-Jacques Pagès. They were offered to the Anton Quartet, a Russian ensemble now based in France.

As for sporting events, Hennessy sponsors the well-known Hennessy Cognac Gold Cup, a traditional English steeplechase, as well as its equivalent in Ireland, and there is also the Hennessy Ladies Cup, one of the most magnificent women's golf tournaments in Europe. Finally, Hennessy has launched publicity campaigns the world over, each with a unique style perfectly matched to the customs and tastes of consumers from different cultural backgrounds.

The resting stag, symbol of the house of Hine.

Hine

MERCHANT
JARNAC (CHARENTE)
1817

The close ties that have existed between cognac and Great Britain is demonstrated once again by the house of Hine, founded by an Englishman and destined to become, fifty years later, English property. Protestantism clearly played a role in its history, and the insatiable English appetite for Charente brandy clearly played a role in its success.

Born in 1775 in Dorset, Thomas Hine came to Jarnac at the age of sixteen to perfect his French. The Hine family maintained cordial relations with a Charente family who, in exchange, dispatched their son to England so he could perfect his English. This was the time of the French Revolution, and Thomas Hine was thrown in jail along with every other subject of the king of England. He remained in jail only a few months and the experience never bothered or embittered him. Shortly after his release, he married Françoise Delamain and thus became a son-in-law of the famous cognac merchant. The house of Delamain was founded in 1763, a date that officially figures in the title of the house of Hine.

Nevertheless, it wasn't until 1817 that Thomas Hine actually founded his own house of cognac, which he set up on the Quai de l'Orangerie on the banks of the Charente River. Later he would become, among other things, mayor of the town of Jarnac—a real success for an immigrant to Charente.

In the great cognac tradition, his descendants would continue his work. They went on to expand operations and increase exports to diverse foreign markets, most notably Great Britain where the family today still enjoys a privileged position.

In 1866, the company went in search of a logo by which it could identify its bottles and barrels and, more important, distinguish itself from the competition and ensure the authenticity of its products. The stag was chosen and some may speculate that this choice was meant to emphasize the name of Hine, given that the word "hind" is phonetically similar. However, the reason for the choice was simpler, as Thomas George Hine's own words attest: "If we need something more than just our name on the cases, why don't we just use a stag." That was back in the days when merchants relied on quality rather than market research to sell their goods.

The line mainly emphasizes higher-quality cognacs, and the Trois Étoiles was a latecomer to the catalogue. The cognacs are largely Grande Champagne origin. The brand's privileged position in Great Britain was consolidated when, in 1962, it was awarded the title of official supplier to the crown, the coveted royal "warrant."

STAG AND ROYAL "WARRANT"

This flattering title, however, was not enough to secure the company against financial difficulty, and it was bought out in 1971 by the British group DCL, the world's leading purveyor of Scotch whiskies. All the same, the founder's descendants, Jacques and Bernard Hine, are still at the helm and are directly involved in the operational decisions concerning the selection and blending of the brandies. The last few years have seen the buyout of DCL by Guinness and the merger between Guinness and LVMH. These events had the benefit of bringing Hennessy and Hine closer together under the same management and joining together their means of production.

For its own part, Hine itself had bought out a few illustrious houses of cognac such as Denis Mounié and Gautier (not to be confused with the house of cognac of that same name from Aigre), which had the distinction of being one of the oldest houses of cognac after Augier.

First and foremost a cultivator and merchant, the house of Hine has always carefully scrutinized the quality of the wines and cognacs provided by its suppliers. To that effect, the company has devised a strict code for assessing the quality of its material and products. This code applies at every step of the production process, and considerable attention is given to the harvest and the fermenting of the grapes, from the careful removal of leaves and the detritus following the pressing to the actual vinification of the juice. A preliminary distillation of a sample of the wine is also carried out as a precaution.

The cognacs are made essentially from brandies of Grande and Petite Champagne origin. The line includes above all the Rare & Delicate, the Antique, and the Triomphe, which is made exclusively of wine of Grande Champagne origin. The house is careful to note the age of the blended brandies and also uses the standard classifications, with the exceptions of the Trois Étoiles, the Signature, and the VSOP.

For a more select group of clients, the Family Réserve is available. This is a specially bottled Grande Champagne (adorned with portraits of successive heads of the house of Hine) and is of limited production. It also comes in a carafe that is sold in an ebony case. Next in line is the Mariage, which comes in a carafe made of Baccarat crystal and sold in a case shaped like a sequoia cone. The case can also be converted into a cigar humidifier. This item was introduced in 1991 to celebrate the two-hundredth wedding anniversary of the founder.

Finally, Hine also specializes in vintage cognacs, intended for the English market. They also offer "early landed" cognacs that have been aged in England before being repatriated to France for bottling. Clearly, Hine has every intention of remaining the most English of the houses of cognac.

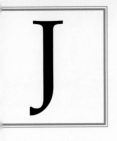

Omer Jullion

WINEGROWER-DISTILLER-MERCHANT

DOMAINE DE MONTIZEAU, SAINT-MAIGRIN (CHARENTE-MARITIME)

The family vineyards and business are located on the chalky hills of the Petite Champagne and Fins Bois areas in the canton of Archiac. The family property covers sixty-nine acres of vines and ninety-nine acres of fields. The Jullion family has been working this land for five generations, and they have their own still and *chais* for aging the cognac.

Under the name of Omer Jullion, an ancestor of the family, the company today is run by Thierry Jullion, and it sells four different kinds of cognac: a Trois Étoiles, a VSOP, a Napoleon, and an XO, as well as 17 ounce bottles of the above. They also make two different pineaux des Charentes, a variety of liqueurs, brandy-based cocktails, and different wines of Charente origin.

Larsen

MERCHANT
COGNAC (CHARENTE)
1926

In 1919, a young Norwegian, Jens Reidar Larsen, left his homeland for Bordeaux in order to set himself up in the wine and spirits trade. A while later, he developed an interest in cognac and in 1926 bought the small producer Joseph Gautier (or Gauthier). Immediately after, he introduced his own brand of cognac. He married a local Cognac girl and had a son, Jean, who is largely responsible for the overseas success of the brand. Today, Frédéric and Nicolas, the grandchildren of the founder, are being groomed to eventually take over the operations.

Quite naturally, he developed his export links with the Scandinavian countries, where cognac, served with water, enjoyed wide popularity. Faithful to their Norwegian origins, the house uses a Viking theme to publicize its products. "Contrary to popular wisdom," Jean is quick to point out, "the Vikings were not barbarians who toured foreign lands, raping, plundering, and pillaging. They

Early on, the house of Larsen used images of its Norwegian ancestry for publicity.

were first and foremost businessmen. They were great travelers, who founded in Kiev the first Russian kingdom. The term 'Viking,' in fact, does not refer to a nation, an ethnic group, or a race but rather to a state of mind, that of the ancient Nordic conquerors who voyaged over the seven seas." Larsen exports to more than eighty countries, with Asia being the principal market. The main market is the duty-free shops in Asia, which account for some fifty percent of Larsen's sales. In order to appeal to Asian tastes, the company sells Fine Champagne cognacs in different colored bottles shaped like Viking longships. The bottles come either in glass or porcelain from Limoges.

The line includes the VS Viking's Cognac, a VSOP, the TVFC (Très Vieille Fine Champagne), a denomination created by Larsen in 1950, the Napoleon, the XO Extra d'Or, and the Extra, aged between 35 and 60 years. The house also exports cognac in bulk to Japan.

Lhéraud

WINEGROWER-DISTILLER-MERCHANT
LASDOUX, NEAR ANGEAC-CHARENTE (CHARENTE)
1881

Alexandre Lhéraud was a winegrower whose origins at Lasdoux date from around 1680. The family farm is on the border between the Petite and Grande Champagne areas. In 1795, Augustin Lhéraud farmed twenty-five acres of vineyards that had been ceded to him by the seigneur de Bouteville as payment to Augustin for maintaining his granary. The granary is still in use today as a warehouse for the house of Lhéraud's cognacs. Eugène Lhéraud, the great-

grandfather of the present owner, significantly expanded the company. In 1875, he inherited as a dowry vineyards in the Grande Champagne area, as well as a sizable lot of aged cognacs. Then in 1881, he installed a still that used wood and coal as fuel. He later became a distiller for a merchant that had England as a principal market.

AN OUTSTANDING VSOP

Between the two world wars, Rémy Lhéraud expanded the estate once again. Guy Lhéraud, who inherited the business from Rémy, decided in 1970 to commercialize cognacs under the family name. He had inherited from his predecessor a substantial stock of fine cognacs, and this enabled him to catapult the name to stardom among connoisseurs and restaura-

teurs. Today, the estate comprises some 123 acres of vineyards in the Petite Champagne area. The vines are of the ugni blanc variety, but also colombard and folle blanche—which is rather rare in Charente.

No flavoring or coloring additives are

included, since they are not necessary—Lhéraud is considered one of the best grower-distillers in the cognac business, a reputation earned in large part from the quality of its VSOP.

The VSOP, like the Cuvées 10 (42% by volume) and the 20 (43% by volume), is sold in a tall bottle with an unusually elegant shape. The line also includes several Petite Champagne cognacs aged between 3 and 20 years, which are sold in traditional cognac bottles.

A few of the cognacs are bottled in reproductions of the old flagons of the eighteenth century. Lhéraud also sells a series of pineaux des Charentes, of which one is absolutely superb, dating from 1959. The company also sells a number of cognac-based liqueurs.

Licorne

WINEGROWER-DISTILLER-MERCHANT
**MALAVILLE, CHÂTEAUNEUF-
SUR-CHARENTE (CHARENTE)**
1815

The vines of the house of Licorne include a small proportion of the folle blanche variety.

The estate is located in Grande Champagne and includes thirty acres of vineyards which have belonged to the same family for about two hundred years. A small lot of the folle blanche variety of grape has been preserved on the estate. The distillation takes place on the premises, in a small still that uses wood and coal as fuel. The aging of the cognac takes place in oak casks with a capacity of eighty gallons which are then stored in *chais*. The bottling also takes place on the premises.

Under the name of Grande Fine Champagne, the house of Licorne sells the VSOP Licorne and the XO Impératrice Joséphine.

The line also includes a Très Vieille Grande Champagne, made from a blend of cognacs dating for the most part from the beginning of the century.

Logis de l'Ajasson

WINEGROWER-DISTILLER-MERCHANT
ÉRAVILLE-CHÂTEAUNEUF
(CHARENTE)

The estate of Logis de l'Ajasson in Grande Champagne.

In 1163, the Abbey of Couronne acquired the estate of Logis de l'Ajasson, where from very early on the monks had established vineyards. Today, it is the name of a vineyard of forty-two acres in Grande Champagne owned by Yves Fillioux. The cognac is entirely the product of the estate and is sold in a bottle of the so-called Norman design, without any indication of age or classification. The Réserve, the Grande Champagne, and the Vieille Réserve are available only on the premises.

Marange

WINEGROWER-DISTILLER-MERCHANT
SAINT-PREUIL (CHARENTE)
1815

Marnier

MERCHANT
BOURG-CHARENTE (CHARENTE)
1827

The estate has been in the family for more than eight generations. It is in the Grande Champagne area and is equipped with its own vineyards, its own distillery, and its own *chais* for vinification and aging. All the same, the company that commercializes this brand also sells a number of different cognacs, all coming from the Grande Champagne area, and sold under the motto of "Art and Passion." Four different classes make up the line: Trois Étoiles, VSOP, Napoleon, and XO.

Storage area where the different brandies are blended.

The Marnier-Lapostolle family bought the château de Bourg, on the banks of the Charente between Jarnac and Cognac, at the beginning of the century. It was built by a page of Henri IV and later belonged to a succession of noble families—Miossens, Salomon, Girac, Camus de Neville—before it was converted into a prison during the French Revolution. Today, it is at this location that the brandies acquired by Marnier-Lapostolle are stored while they age.

The line is not extensive but includes three cognacs: the Marnier, which is very aromatic due to the prevalence of Borderies in the blend; the VSOP Fine Champagne, and the XO of Grande Champagne.

The company Marnier-Lapostolle is better known for the famous liqueur Grand Marnier, a cognac and orange-based liqueur. The company nevertheless remains true to its origins as a Charente brandy producer by selling a very interesting line of cognacs. The distillery, originally at Neauphle-le-Château, was founded by Jean-Baptiste Lapostolle in 1827. It was a nondescript brandy in comparison to its competitors until the war of 1870. The German invasion obliged Eugène Lapostolle, the founder's son, to flee to Charente. There, he discovered cognac and acquired a nice stock of his own.

Nevertheless, it was his son-in-law, Louis-Alexandre Marnier-Lapostolle, who put the cognac to better use by developing the orange and cognac-based liqueur.

At the time, a number of orange liqueurs already existed (also called curaçao), but the liqueur of Marnier-Lapostolle was destined to outdo them all, thanks to its use of cognacs of Grande and Petite Champagne origin.

The success of Grand Marnier Cordon Rouge rapidly grew, especially overseas on the export markets. Over a number of years, the brand would go on to win first prize at the expositions of French liqueur exporters.

Martell

WINEGROWER-DISTILLER-MERCHANT
COGNAC (CHARENTE)
1715

Jean Martell was born in Jersey in March 1694, into a family known on the island since the thirteenth century. His father was an important merchant and navigator, but he died five months before the birth of his son. Jean began by learning about business from a merchant in Guernsey. The Channel Islands played an important role at the time in trade (or smuggling, depending on the political winds of the period) between England and the Continent. Barely twenty-one years old, Jean Martell decided to strike out on his own and so headed for France to set himself up as a merchant. He first began working with a partner who lived in Bordeaux, but who, like himself, was originally from Jersey. Like many merchants of the time, he dabbled in the buying and selling of a variety of goods. Brandy was one of his mainstays but he also imported coal, wool, linen, flour, and even dresses from England. He later turned to tea, coffee, tobacco, silk, and beer after he discovered the extensive Dutch trade with Asia. The business was not a success, however, and it folded. Nevertheless, he eventually managed to pay off his debts and set himself up again.

In 1726, he married Jeanne Brunet, daughter of an important merchant family in Cognac, and moved to Cognac, where

he lived in the Gatebourse quarter beside the Charente. Jeanne died young and Jean Martell remarried. His new wife was Rachel Lallemand, who also belonged to an old, established family from the town. She was Catholic and Jean was obliged to renounce his Protestantism.

At his death in 1753, he left his widow a thriving business, which she ran in partnership with her brother and later with her sons Jean and Frédéric. At the time of the Revolution, Martell was one of the largest businesses in town, exporting cognac to the United States (1784) and Russia (1803). It was also one of the first to sell its products under its own name. The Martells, who had become important public and political figures, dominated the cognac trade throughout the nineteenth century. Following the phylloxera crisis, the company entirely revamped its production methods. With its mounting stocks of cognac, Martell went into distilling wine, and around 1880, built enormous complexes at Cognac that were nothing short of factories for the production of brandy. The distillery included four stills, each with a capacity of 158 gallons (the average capacity of a still at that time was 26 gallons), and the first *chai* they built for blending cognac could hold up to fifty barrels with a capacity of 4,620 gallons each. Another one held up to thirty-six barrels, with a total capacity of 166,320 gallons, joined by nearly two miles of pipes. It was a tour de force that must have impressed the competition, and in 1892, an issue of the periodical, *Revue périodique,* elevated Martell to the status of an industrial enterprise.

CONQUERING THE WORLD

In the middle of the nineteenth century a number of new markets were emerging, notably in Australia in 1851, China in 1861, and Japan in 1868. Still, the competition was stiff, especially from such giants as Hennessy. At stake for these two companies was nothing less than world domination of the cognac trade. The two families nevertheless had

Pierre Martell.

intimate ties. Jacques Hennessy, for example, had married Marthe Martell at the end of the eighteenth century, while Jean-Gabriel Martell married Marie Hennessy. It was, all the same, at the level of commerce that the ties between the two companies were closest. A price-fixing agreement was reached between the two companies and it lasted for decades. This agreement constituted, in effect, a duopoly of the cognac trade that endured until the end of World War II. The purpose was not to enhance each company's cognac revenues so much as to thwart any challenge to the companies' control of the market. It also protected the economic interests of the entire region. The Martells, for example, were staunch defenders of the rights of independent distillers throughout the region.

The male descendants of Jean Martell were to maintain control of the company until the death of Edouard in 1920. The marriage of his sister, Marie-Mathilde, to Paul Firino led to the creation of a new family branch, the Firino-Martell.

Today, Patrick Firino-Martell, of the eighth generation, heads the company.

In order to accommodate the financial needs created by the expanding market of the last half of the twentieth century, the company's capital was destined to change hands. In 1988, the company was finally bought out by the Canadian corporation Seagrams. Seagrams, founded by Sam Bronfman, had for a long time tried to gain a foothold in Cognac by buying the house of Augier twenty years earlier, but that venture did not work out.

THE ART OF MARTELL

Seagrams needed to own a few prestigious cognac brand names with large holdings to secure its dominance of the world market for spirits. Hennessy had already fallen under the dominion of Guinness a year earlier when the LVMH group was formed. Courvoisier was already owned by Allied-Lyons. Martell's independence was certain not to last much longer.

The British group IDV-Grand Met had

The Martell coat of arms depicts a stylized bird and is found on all of the house's bottles.

already attempted a takeover of Martell, but it was Seagrams who finally succeeded, at a heavy price, in winning out. This submission to the Seagrams group rapidly led to radical changes in the objectives and methods of Martell. New products were introduced, and the marketing and commercial strategies and methods were completely overhauled in 1990 under the generic name of the "Art of Martell." The campaign was launched from the Eiffel Tower by Edgar Bronfman Jr. himself.

At first, the Art of Martell campaign implemented twenty-two publicity visuals under the themes "Savoir-Faire" and "Art de Vivre." Alongside these more commercial approaches, Martell also sponsored different cultural events, notably in the areas of art and music. The first took place in 1990 in Paris and featured the celebrated tenor Placido Domingo. Other events took place in the United States with such luminaries from the music world as Daniel Barenboim, Sir Georg Solti, and Zubin Mehta. In October of 1992, Martell co-sponsored an exhibition in Japan of the paintings of Maurice Utrillo. The company also organizes a yearly exhibition at its headquarters in Cognac.

The takeover by Seagrams also led to a massive influx of capital that was used to invest in increasing production. Thus, new *chais* with a total capacity of 40,000 barrels were built at Chanteloup and construction was begun on a new distillery at Gallienne, in the Borderies area, which was hailed as the biggest and most modern in the region. Finally, the line of cognacs was revamped and enlarged.

Martell had been one of the first houses to make a distinction between its various cognacs. In 1800, the name Martell was branded on the casks, followed by the introduction of a new class of cognac in 1819, the Extra, first mentioned in a letter from Théodore Martell to a client in London that accompanied fifteen barrels of cognac. In 1831, the company first exported a VSOP class of cognac and from 1843 on, the bottles were engraved with the name "J. & F. Martell." In 1912, the Cordon Bleu was introduced and it was an immediate success worldwide. It was to be followed by the Cordon d'Argent in 1923. The aromatic and florid taste was due to the cognac's Borderies origins, of which Martell procures some sixty percent of the harvest. It eventually went on to become a signature of the Martell style.

Today, Martell exports about 1.8 million cases of cognac each year to some 140 countries. That accounts for 98% of its production. The company owns 667 acres of vineyards, which supply only 3% of its needs. To make up the difference, some 2,300 winegrowers-distillers are under contract to the company. In addition to its new complex at Gardenne, the company employs some 13 other distilleries which produce only for Martell.

The company uses only casks made from oak from the Tronçais forest, preferred for its hard grain and low tannin content. Oak from Limousin is used only to repair either damaged or old casks. On the occasion of the company's 280th anniversary, the home of the founder, Jean Martell, dubbed the "Coquille," was restored. Julian Bly, an interior decorator and specialist of eighteenth-century design, re-created in exact detail the lifestyle of a merchant from the period, redecorating everything from the office to the kitchen.

Martell sells the following classes of cognac, each without exception a blend of the four best areas (Grande Champage, Petite Champagne, Borderies, and Fins Bois):

• VS Fine Cognac.

• VSOP Médallion.

• Napoleon Spécial Réserve, launched in 1990, mainly sold in duty-free shops.

• Noblige, launched in 1994 and sold in a bottle of very contemporary design.

• Cordon Bleu, the great classic.

• XO Suprème, made only of brandies from Martell's own vineyards.

• Extra, a blend of very old brandies from the above four areas.

• Classique, a blend of brandies that are more than 40 years old and sold since 1953 in a Baccarat crystal carafe. This name was not used until 1993.

• L'Or de J. & F. Martell, introduced in 1992 and sold in duty-free shops and a limited number of luxury boutiques. It is a blend of old brandies sold in an original carafe with a 24-carat gold plated shoulder.

• Gobelet Royal, in a carafe made of blue Limoges porcelain. It is sold exclusively in the duty-free shops throughout the Far East.

The estate of de la Motte is a typical example of traditional Charente architecture.

Documents from 1660 bear witness that relatives of Nicolas Ménard were already *laboreurs à bras* (farmhands) who owned *treuil et chaudières,* or a wine press and a still. They lived at Salles-d'Angles in the Grande Champagne area. The lineage extends uninterrupted into the present generation. The existence of Jean Ménard

Maurin

WINEGROWER
SAINT-DIZANT-DU-GUA
(CHARENTE-MARITIME)
XVIIIth CENTURY

The Domaine de la Motte, located in the far south of the Charente-Maritime and technically in the Fins Bois area, has been cultivated for over two centuries. The fifty-four acres are largely devoted to grapes for use in distilling cognac, of which there are five classes, and in the making of pineaux des Charentes. The traditional Charente-style building was expanded in 1901 with the addition of a pavillion. The premises also include *chais* of very old construction. Jean-Paul Maurin, the owner, sells about 52,800 gallons directly or to other outlets.

Ménard

WINEGROWER-DISTILLER-MERCHANT
SAINT-MÊME-LES-CARRIÈRES
(CHARENTE)
1815

Though the company that oversees production at Ménard dates only to 1946, the family origins are considerably older.

is also documented. In 1815, he owned a large vineyard and was in the distilling business.

Today, the Ménard family owns five different estates covering a total area of 198 acres in the Grande Champagne area. The company was created after World War II by Jean-Paul Ménard and his two children. Their goal was to commercialize their own cognacs rather than sell them to other merchants, as had been done in the past. Today, four members of the family own all of the company's stock, and they sell only their own products.

The line includes five cognacs: the Sélection des Domaines, aged 2 to 5 years; a VSOP, aged 4 to 10 years; the Napoleon, aged 20 to 25 years; the XO, aged about 35 years, with 42% alcohol by volume; the Ancestrale, aged about 50 years, with 45% alcohol by volume.

Ménard also sells three different pineaux: a white, a rose, and a Très Vieux Blanc, which has been aged in oak casks for over 10 years.

Menuet

WINEGROWER-DISTILLER-MERCHANT
SAINT-MÊME-LES-CARRIÈRES
(CHARENTE)
1850

A census of 1680 records that Menuet was cultivating a vineyard near Cognac at that time. The vineyard in cultivation today, in Grande Champagne, dates back to 1850, when Louis Menuet purchased his first twelve acres. His grandson, Ernest, won a gold medal at the 1900 World Exposition in Paris. Twenty years later, he began selling his own cognac in bottles, a rarity in those days for a distiller.

Today, the estate includes 111 acres of ugni blanc vines, and is under the direction of Marie-Josette Menuet and her husband, Michel Croizet. Their son, David Croizet, and his wife, Christine, are in charge of sales. The wine is distilled in the presence of the dregs, and the brandy is aged for a year in new casks before being transferred to the "red" casks. The alcohol reduction is done by using distilled water until the alcohol is diluted to fifty percent by volume, and then further titrated until the alcohol content is forty percent by volume.

A medal awarded at the Universal Exposition of 1900.

Sixty percent of the production is exported. The Menuet line of cognacs includes a VSOP, aged 5 years; an XO; an Extra, aged more than 20 years; and the Hors d'Âge, aged at least 40 years. The house also offers several pineaux, of which the 5-year-old and the 10-year-old are wonderful. In 1993, Menuet won a silver medal for its XO at the London competition for wines and spirits.

Meukow

COMMERCIAL BRAND
COGNAC (CHARENTE)
1862

The Meukow brothers, Auguste-Christophe and Gustave, were of German origin and originally from Silesia. They arrived in France around 1850 after being sent by the czar of Russia to select and purchase cognac for his court. A few years later they started their own house of cognac in partnership first with M. Lervoire and later with Henry Bouraud, who was mayor of Cognac.

The Meukow brothers benefited from substantial commercial contacts in Russia and Scandinavia, and consequently their business was an immediate success. They became noted for the subtle blends used in producing their cognacs.

At the end of the nineteenth century, Gustave Kleabish (or Klaebisch) took over from the Meukow brothers as head of the company. At the outbreak of World War I, his German origins cost him the company, which was confiscated in 1914. During World War II, the tide would turn and a Klaebisch became the Nazi governor of the region. However, bearing no grudge, he made no effort to recover the family business. In the meantime, Meukow had become the property of the Sheperd family, who expanded exports to other countries, notably the United States. Following World War II, André Villesuzanne, a son-in-law of the Sheperd family, inherited the Meukow properties. He already owned a substantial vineyard in the Petite Champagne area at Salignac, which also included a distillery.

The reputation of Meukow cognac continued to rise, especially overseas, and the house eventually became the official supplier to the House of Lords in London, the White House in Washington, and various European courts.

In 1979, Michel Coste, the former director of the house of Otard, bought Meukow. Two years later, he founded the Compagnie Commerciale de Guyenne. He completely modified the marketing of the brand to make it the flagship of the group, especially overseas. His approach was to give cognac a more concrete and credible image in contrast to the image of sophistication and high class favored by the other makers. To do so, he employed the image of a leopard, the "mark of a feline," to distinguish the bottles. The line offers three types of cognac: VSOP, MPC or Napoleon, and XO. The cognacs are sold mainly in duty-free stores throughout the Far East at fairly reasonable prices. The Chinese have given the Meukow brand a nickname—the "Jin Bao," or golden leopard. The company has also bought several other houses of cognac which had run into difficulties, companies such as Royer-Guillet, L. Brugerolle, Lucien Foucauld, Réau-Richard, and others. In addition to the stocks and diverse means of production, these acquistions have permitted the group to penetrate other markets such as the mass market in France.

Monier-Ferrand

WINEGROWER-DISTILLER-MERCHANT
SEGONZAC (CHARENTE)
1993

The problems between Pierre Ferrand and the major shareholders of "Pierre Ferrand" have already been discussed in an earlier chapter. Having fared poorly in the conflict, Pierre Ferrand was led to commercialize his own cognac. To do so, he gave a partnership another try and went into business with Franck G. Monier, creating the brand Monier-Ferrand.

Pierre Ferrand hails from a very old Charente family who lived in or near La Nérolle next to Segonzac. A certain Émery Ferran, a family ancestor, was in the wine business as early as 1469; and the first distiller in the family, Jacques Ferrand, got his license in 1702, according to the local archives. Easily recognized by the ever-present beret, Pierre Ferrand is the twelfth generation of his family to ply the trade of distiller.

The Monier family dates back to the eighteenth century at Chassors, a small

The village of Saint-Preuil, near Segonzac, in Champagne.

town along the banks of the Charente. The family went into the cognac business in 1921 when they began producing cognac from just under ten acres of vineyards in Fins Bois. In 1984, Franck Monier took over the business and substantially expanded it. Today, it covers nearly ninety-nine acres spread between the

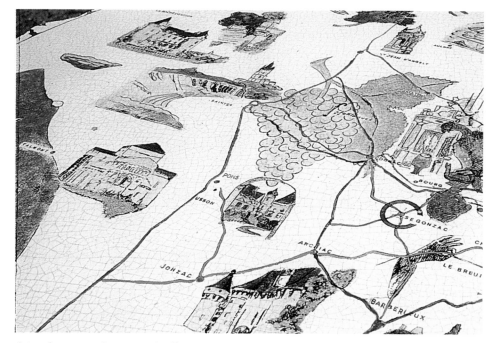

A tourist map at Segonzac, in Charente.

Grande Champagne area near Segonzac and the Fins Bois area near Chassors and Luchac.

Under the brand name "Famille Ferrand," the company sells cognacs from Grande Champagne: Prestige, aged 10 years, with a white label; the Réserve de la Propriété, aged 15 years; the Sélection des Anges, aged 30 years, sold in the traditional cognac bottle; and finally the Réserve Ancestrale, aged 60 years, in a hand-blown glass carafe. Three Grande Champagne cognacs are also sold under the brand name of "Paul Monier:" the Initiale, aged 10 years; the Vintage, aged 20 years; and the Extra, aged 30 years. Also sold are a couple of pineaux aged 5 years (white and rose) and one aged 10 years.

Montifaud

WINEGROWER-DISTILLER-MERCHANT
JARNAC-CHAMPAGNE
(CHARENTE-MARITIME)
XVIIIth CENTURY.

Château Montifaud produces four principal classes of cognac: the VS, aged 5 years; the VSOP, aged 10 years; the Napoleon, aged 15 to 18 years; and the XO, aged 27 to 30 years, with 40% alcohol by volume. In addition to the classic "rustic" bottle, the cognac is sold in a variety of containers:

• The Jarnacaise, a tall bottle with a volume of 17 ounces and used for the VS, VSOP, and the XO;

• The Roland, a bottle with a sloping

The Vallet family has owned the Château Montifaud for several generations. There is no precise date available, but the oldest extant documents concerning the family date to the eighteenth century. The vineyards, covering some 123 acres, are located in the Petite Champagne area, in a sector where Campanian chalk is particularly prevalent. This house is one of the rare ones to employ the term "château" to designate its products. There are fewer than twenty Charente vineyards that make use of the term, while over three hundred brands of cognac are registered.

The Vallet family maintains a stock of very old cognacs, which include:

• Eight bottles of cognac distilled in 1830 by Pierre Vallet, the great-grandfather of today's owner, Louis Vallet.

• A batch of cognacs produced by Maurice Vallet at the end of the last century and at the beginning of this century. They are stored in demijohns and sold in hand-blown glass bottles.

Moreover, nine casks, each containing 1,135 gallons of cognac distilled from the 1989 harvest, have been officially sealed by the *Bureau national interprofessionel de cognac.* They are being stored over the next several years before being sold as a vintage cognac. The Château Monifaud has managed to maintain the exquisit floral characteristics of its cognacs of Petite Champagne origin by using only its own harvest and special methods of fermentation, distillation, and alcohol reduction.

form used for the VS, VSOP, and the XO;

• The Futura, a tall bottle with a reproduction on the label of *Les Fantastiques,* a painting by Serge Van Kache (for VSOP and XO).

• The Ancestrale, a round bottle that is hand-blown and used for the XO and the Héritage Louis Vallet, a cognac from 1942 and containing 42% alcohol by volume. These top of the line classes of cognac are also available in carafes made of Arques or Sèvres crystal.

Moyet

MERCHANT
COGNAC (CHARENTE)
1864

This house is something of a "sleeping beauty." It maintains some superb stocks of high-quality cognac, which have been deftly resurrected by a new generation of merchants who have shown once and for all that there is no single formula for success in the world of cognac.

Émile Moyet was originally a winegrower. He created a limited company in 1864, an unusual organization for that period, in order to sell his brandies. Its story is actually not that different from other small- and medium-sized houses of cognac that were established back then. If Moyet has enjoyed the accolades of many admirers at home and abroad, it is perhaps more notable for a characteristic that is even more unusual. For more than seventy years, the same man, Honoré Piquepaille was the cellar master, super-

The entrance to a typical Charente farm often includes two passages of different sizes.

tion. To do so, Pierre Dubarry changed the marketing approach and set about establishing a more exclusive clientele that includes fine restaurants and wine and spirits specialists. These superb cognacs met with immediate success. Moyet gained a reputation for being a purveyor of old, rare cognacs and became something of a media celebrity. The house became the favorite supplier of an elite clientele throughout the world.

Though profiting from its reputation worthy of a house of haute couture, Moyet nevertheless produces a more reasonably priced line of cognacs, sold in bulk to fine restaurants and specialty boutiques. This is an entirely new kind of approach, the niche which had been overlooked by the larger companies.

vising the blending and aging of the house's different cognacs. The consequence has been a steady accumulation of stocks of an impressive quality. Honoré Piquepaille entered the business as an apprentice and shortly after the World War II went on to become the owner of Moyet. However, this indisputable expert on cognac was somewhat less talented when it came to management and sales. The house had only modest sales and its reputation rapidly began to decline.

In 1980, Moyet was sold to a group of stockholders, one of whom was Marie-France Chabrerie (Honoré's grand niece); her husband, Marc-George; Pierre Dubarry and a few other people. Since then the company's capital has changed hands, but Pierre Dubarry, a former executive of the firm Solex, has become one of the most tireless promoters of Moyet. The new team initially opted for the more classical strategy of focusing on the mass markets and duty-free boutiques. But the results fell short of expectations largely as a result of the price-fixing agreements made between the larger companies, which effectively locked out the competition.

So, in 1985, the team settled on a new strategy that involved exploiting the sizable stocks of fine cognac it had accumulated during almost a century of produc-

The preference for quantity over quality has left the larger companies largely indifferent to the subtler aspects of—most notably—their cognac products.

Instead of harboring ambitions of conquering the Japanese or Chinese markets, Moyet has proven that a house of cognac can thrive by concentrating on French markets, such as restaurants. The irrepressible Pierre Dubarry visits the restaurateurs and has induced many of them to offer small doses of cognac to their customers. His hope is that this will revive the habit of the after-dinner digestif. Imitated by many others, Moyet brought back into fashion the traditional cognac bottle with the wax seal over the cork, a common practice now.

The line offered by the house principally offers the following cognacs:

• A Petite Champagne, aged over 7 years.

• A Fine Champagne, aged over 10 years.

• A Grande Champagne, aged over 30 years and with an uncut alcohol content of 53.6% by volume.

• A Fine Champagne XO, a blend of brandable cognacs: brandies dating between 1932 and 1973.

For the more extravagant consumer, the house's special reserves, of a limited production, are also available:

• The Tonneau No. 1, or Extra, a blend of the four best *crus*, aged between 25 and 80 years;

• The Tonneau No. 19, Très Vieille Fine Champagne, from 1902 to 1964;

• The Tonneau No. 8, Très Vieille Fine Champagne, aged between 40 to 85 years.

• The Fut No. 3, Très Vieille Fine Champagne, made with brandies from 1848, 1858 and 1906: "very fine, strong yet moderate, full of aroma."

• The Fut No. 2, Très Vieille Fine Champagne, aged 80 to 140 years: "lightly woody, very ample, harmonious with a fine lingering aftertaste."

Normandin-Mercier

MERCHANT

LA PÉRAUDIÈRE, DOMPIERRE-SUR-MER (CHARENTE-MARITIME)

1872

Jules Normandin, originally a wine broker and landowner at Cognac, started his own cognac business in 1872, and soon after he was looking for a new location for the *chais*. It had to be near a train station and a river port, to ship the brandy and import the coal used to fire the stills. In 1885, Jules Normandin finally bought the château de la Péraudière at Dompierre-sur-Mer, located beside a canal that in 1885 led to La Rochelle. From 1945 to 1978, the commercial activity of the house consisted solely in the selling of old cognacs in casks to established houses of cognac.

After the death of Georges Normandin in 1977, the family estate was divided between his two children, with the land going to his daughter and the family business going to his son, Jean-Marie, representing to the fourth generation.

The house produces top-of-the-line cognacs from Grande and Petite Champagne; seventy-five percent of the production is exported to Europe and the United States, with the rest sold mostly to restaurants. Connoisseurs appreciate its quality and authenticity. The cognacs are aged in old "red" casks, and the alcohol content is reduced slowly with diluted cognac (five percent each year), to retain the specific characteristics of each cognac. Like the Vieille Fine Champagne, aged fifteen years, the two cognacs are aged separately in small 92-gallon casks, then blended and stored in larger barrels of 145 gallons. They are then aged slowly.

Normandin-Mercier sells a mellow and ample Grande Champagne Réserve that is aged thirty years. They also sell the Petite Champagne Vieille and Grande Champagne Vieille, aged about twenty years. These are unblended, the alcohol is not reduced and they are bottled only on demand. Next is the Très Vieille Grande Champagne, seventy years old and a real jewel, with a very subtle flavor and a marvelous aftertaste.

Still largely unknown, perhaps because it left the Cognac environs, Normandin-Mercier bears witness to the quality that can be attained by an independent producer with a solid tradition in cognac.

Otard

MERCHANT
COGNAC (CHARENTE)
1795

This name, famous throughout the world of cognac, has origins that go far back. The story begins with the Vikings, in 849 to be exact. That was the year that the "Jarl" (Lord) Ottard, a Viking chief, settled on the French island of Noirmoutier after having been forced off his lands in Norway. He shows up again later in history in the service of Alfred the Great, king of England. Later, he would return to France and resettle near Bray; and then in 911, his adventurous days came to an end during an expedition in England.

His grandson, Hugues, accompanied William the Conqueror to England, where he fought at the battle of Hastings and was rewarded with two English fiefdoms. The Norman branch of the Ottard line disappeared in the thirteenth century, but the English branch endured, having established itself in Scotland, south of Dundee. In 1561, William Ottard married Helen of Kirkaldy de la Grange, a name that later would see service as a well-known brand of cognac.

The family was loyal to the Stuarts; and in 1688, James Otard de la Grange followed James II into exile in France. There, he enlisted in the service of Louis XIV and distinguished himself in various military campaigns. In appreciation of his services, he was made a baron and a knight of Saint-Louis in 1701. His son Jacques settled in Périgord in 1760; some of his sons later settled in Angoumois, near Cognac, where the family went into the business of brandy.

In December of 1773, Jean-Baptiste Antoine Otard de la Grange, James Otard's great-grandson, was born in Chérac. He was educated at the military school of Pontlevoy, where he graduated as an engineer. He remained true to his Catholic faith and loyal to the king, which put him in conflict with the new authorities in charge of the Terror. He was imprisoned at Saintes in 1792 and sentenced to death, but was rescued from execution when the local inhabitants managed to spirit him out of prison the night before. He fled to England but decided to return to France two years later, where he was determined to return to the cognac trade. His family held ample stocks that had been accumulated over thirty years. He went into partnership with the nearby distillers, Jean and Léon Dupuy, and together they began the production and marketing of their own cognac.

The house of Otard-Dupuy was founded in 1795. A year later, it bought the château in Cognac, a former royal that had been nationalized and put up for sale. Construction on the château began in the eleventh century, but the bulk of it was built during the thirteenth century by the Lusigna. It was returned to the count Jean de Valois, who continued construction on it from 1450. It is there, in 1494, that François de Valois was born. The future François I spent his childhood there, and in later life, never tired of embellishing and restoring the premises, which he often visited.

The château was largely neglected by François' descendants. In the eighteenth century, it was even put to use as a prison. The count of Artois, the future Charles X, was the château's last owner before Baron Otard acquired it. Baron Otard no doubt appreciated the château's thick walls, its cellars, and its numerous floors, all of which would be excellent for aging cognac. The variations in humidity from floor to floor had the added benefit that a whole variety of different cognacs could be produced on the same premises.

INTERNATIONAL GROWTH

Jean-Baptiste Otard was quick to exploit his numerous relations and connections in England to promote sales of his cognacs, while managing to slip through the blockade imposed by Napoleon. He was popular with the citizenry, and in 1804 became mayor of Cognac, remaining in office until his death in 1824, except for the period of Napoleon's return, known as the Hundred Days. Jean-Baptiste was also twice elected deputy to the National Assembly. His private home became the present town hall in 1892.

After his death, his partner, Léon Dupuy, became the director of the company. He would later go into partnership

Right: the royal château at Cognac. It was bought by the house of Otard after the Revolution.

with Jean-Baptiste's children, William and Léon. The company began to grow rapidly, eventually challenging Hennessy and Martell as the third-largest producer of cognac in the mid-nineteenth century. Today, the descendants of Otard and Dupuy still manage the company, ever in search of new markets to conquer. Count Henri de Castellane, a son-in-law of Auguste Otard, became involved in running the company, as did his son, the Viscount Boni de Castellane.

René Otard, the last direct descendant of the founding father, died in May 1934. The Ramefort family had nevertheless already taken control of the business by

J.A. OTARD KEITH de LA GRANGE
Député de la Charente, Maire de Cognac
Officier de la Légion d'Honneur, Commandeur de S.Grégoire...

The baron Jean-Baptiste Otard was mayor of Cognac during the Empire.

1930. As for the Dupuys, they have not participated on the company's board since the Liberation of France. Once a power to be reckoned with, the company has fallen behind the times and lost some of its former luster. For example, Otard had for years refused to sell its cognacs in bottles, dismissing such a practice as appropriate to "grocers," even though the competition had readily adopted the practice to good effect.

Martini & Rossi shook some sense into the house, half asleep in its medieval château. After several initial offers and partial buyouts, Martini took over in 1991, combining Otard with its other acquistions, Château de Lagrange and Exshaw. The new operation was called Château de Cognac SA. The Château de Cognac itself is worth a visit. Many of the rooms have been restored and other renovations are continuing. The rooms currently welcoming visitors are the governor's abode, dating from the fifteenth century; the armory, dating from the thirteenth century; the room with the bas-reliefs representing the battle of Marignan and the meeting at the camp of the

Drap d'Or; and the Renaissance guards' quarters and hall, which rests on the foundations of the old walls of the city. The walls of these rooms are more than six feet thick and maintain a constant humidity. The *paradis* is located there, and this is where the house of Otard stores its oldest goods, notably one lot dating back to 1820.

The line today, strongly classical, includes a VS, VSOP Fine Champagne, Napoleon (aged up to 15 years), an XO (aged up to 35 years), and the Extra (aged 50 years or more). Most of the cognacs are sold in a superbly shaped bottle that is long and elegant. They are very typical of the house of Otard and immediately recognizable to any cognac consumer.

The guards' quarters at the Château de Cognac (above), and the *paradis* at the house of Otard; in addition to its historical interest, the château is also perfect for aging cognac.

Paulet

MERCHANT
COGNAC (CHARENTE)
1848

This company was established in 1848 by Jean-Maurice Lacroux on cognac-producing property active since the eighteenth century. Today, the house of Paulet belongs to the Cointreau family (Frapin). Nevertheless, the great-grandsons of the founder, Bernard and Jacques Lacroux, are still involved in the direction of the company to this day.

The extensive line of cognacs offered by this house is nonetheless remarkable for its almost exclusive use of brandies of Borderies origin. The emphasis on Borderies is symbolized by the cuvée Borderies Très Vieilles. A story has it that an American restaurateur, desiring to put the expertise of Pierre Troisgros to the test, had him taste a cognac blind. The French chef immediately recognized the Borderies Très Vieilles of Château Paulet due to its unusual floral aromas.

The house has also won a number of awards for its cognacs, including a gold medal for its XO at the international wine and spirits competition in London in 1993. It also won the coveted Cyril Ray trophy for the best cognac that same year.

Entrance to the Paulet property.

Having benefited from a newly designed series of bottles, the line offered by Château Paulet is divided into three categories:

• The Écusson Rouge, the VSOP, and the Cuvée Supérieur.

• The Napoleon, the XO Fine Champagne, and the Extra, sold in a bottle with a distinctively long neck.

• The special presentations in carafes of Sèvres crystal (Fine Champagne Louis XVI), by Lalique (Very Rare), or in flagons made of porcelain from Limoges, one of which is shaped like the Louvre pyramid.

In 1994, for the 500th birthday of François I, the house sold the Réserve Cristal François I, a limited series of no more than 500 crystal carafes.

Château Paulet is also known for the quality of its pineaux des Charentes.

Harvest at André Petit in the 1960s.

André Petit

WINEGROWER-DISTILLER-MERCHANT
BERNEUIL (CHARENTE)
1965

Some time in the middle of the last century, a certain Goulard, a wealthy weaver, decided to invest part of his capital in a vineyard. He also invested in the installation of a distillery and went into the cognac-producing business with the help of his cousin, who was a distiller at the house of Hennessy. For decades, the distilled brandy was sold exclusively to Hennessy.

In 1921, one of Goulard's granddaughters married Albert Petit. From that time on, the company bore his name. In 1965, Albert Petit's son, André, who had succeeded his father as head of the business, decided to break away from Hennessy and sell the cognac himself. Today, the estate includes thirty acres of vineyards in the Fins Bois and Bons Bois areas. One of the stills that is used today dates to 1873.

The line includes a Trois Étoiles, a VSOP (aged 8 to 10 years), the Napoleon Vieille Réserve (aged 15 to 20 years), the XO Très Rare, which won a silver medal at the world brandy contest of 1990, and the Hors d'Âge, a blend of cognacs aged 80 years or older. It is sold either in bottles or in carafes. The house also produces a pineau blanc (aged 6 years) and a pineau rosé, which have won a number of honors in various competitions.

Prince Hubert de Polignac

WINEGROWER-DISTILLER-MERCHANT
COGNAC (CHARENTE)
1947

The movement toward forming agricultural cooperatives was never a significant force in Charente. In 1929, a few winegrowers formed a cooperative to combat declining revenues. Two years later, they took the name Unicoop, a company that enabled them to export their products. Led notably by Pierre-Lucien Lucquiaud, the company encountered difficulties almost from the start, difficulties that were largely due to the economic crisis between the two world wars.

Nevertheless, in 1947, a break came that allowed them to sell their best cognacs under the name Prince Hubert de Polignac. This is the name of one of the oldest families of the French nobility, whose origins date back to the ninth century in Auvergne.

Over the centuries, the Polignac family provided France with soldiers, ambassadors, and provincial governors. Jules de Polignac, a minister under Charles X, was made a prince in 1822 by Pope Pius VII and by King Louis XVIII. One of his descendants, Hubert de Polignac, agreed to lend his name to the line of cognacs. As a marketing consultant in France and abroad, he made significant contributions to establishing the brand on the market. He worked tirelessly to promote the brand until his death in a car accident in 1981.

Today, the Unicoop cooperative includes around one thousand winegrowers. This accounts for some 7,400 acres of vineyards, twenty percent in Grande and Petite Champagne, forty-five percent in Fins Bois, and thirty-five percent in Bons Bois. Unicoop employs eleven distilleries, including sixty stills, producing 6.6 million gallons of wine each year, and twenty *chais* to age the brandy and stock up to the equivalent of 28 million bottles.

In 1969, Unicoop took control of Henri Mounier, a merchant house founded in Cognac in 1858. The infrastructure acquired with the house of Mounier is used today to commercialize the wines and spirits produced by Unicoop.

The headquarters of Unicoop, owners of the brand Prince Hubert de Polignac.

The Prince Hubert de Polignac line makes up the group's main products. It includes a Trois Étoiles, the VSOP (aged 10 years on average), the Napoleon (aged about 15 years), the Top Old Pale (aged 12 years on average), the XO Royal (aged an average of 20 years), the Dynastie de Grande Champagne (35 to 60 years old), and several models sold in crystal carafes and carafes of Limoges porcelain. The company also sells other brands of cognac, such as the Prince Michel de Bourbon, Comte de Ipanema, Paul Bocuse, and Henri Mounier. Still others are made for mass distribution throughout France, such as the Grande Monarque, de Chabrac, de Bonnefont, La Fayette, Paysans Charentais, etc. Unicoop is the largest cognac producer on the French market and sells more than 6 million bottles each year. Nevertheless, 70% of its production is sold in more than 85 countries.

The group also makes a number of pineaux des Charentes, the leading brand of Charente wine, Reynac, and an assortment of other brandies and spirits (Brunot, de Pourvil, Villemin). The company also produces an armagnac, a calvados, and an orange-based cognac liqueur.

R

Raymond Ragnaud

WINEGROWER-DISTILLER-MERCHANT
LE CHÂTEAU, AMBLEVILLE (CHARENTE)
1920

Paul Ragnaud went into business as a winegrower and distiller in 1920 in the heart of the Grande Champagne area at the château d'Ambleville. In 1941, his son Raymond took over the responsibilities of overseeing the vineyards and began to commercialize the superb cognacs made by his father. In 1960, he bought a new vineyard at Criteuil. Following his death in 1963, his wife kept the family business operating with the help of her two children, Jean-Marie Ragnaud and Françoise Bricq. The estate today covers 109 acres of land, where mainly ugni blanc but some folle blanche vines are grown. It is unusual in Charente, but a woman, Françoise Bricq, is in charge of aging the brandy and the blending of the different cognacs. In the opinion of many, her cognacs without a doubt include some of the most perfectly balanced available and are not to be missed.

Right: the banks of the Charente.

,The line of cognacs offered by Raymond Ragnaud is one of the most complete on the market and includes many varieties of Grande Champagne origin. Included in the line are:

• Selection (40% alcohol by volume), aged 3 to 4 years.

• Réserve, aged 7 years: "with a mellow nuance of vanilla."

• Vieille Réserve (41%), aged 15 years: "a delicate and fine aroma."

• Réserve Rare (41%), aged 18 years: "refreshing, sharp and harmonious."

• Grande Réserve (44%), aged 15 years, owes its clear color, floral aroma, and grape flavor to the old casks in which it is aged.

• Extra Vieux (42%), aged 25 years: "vanilla accents, elegant, well balanced."

• Hors d'Âge (43%), aged 35 years: "rich and aromatic."

• Très Vieille Grande Champagne (50%), from 1952, by Raymond Ragnaud: "releases on the palate a mellow, supple and persistent aromatic richness."

• Héritage (45%) distilled at the beginning of the century by Paul Ragnaud: "has attained perfection in terms of balance, complexity and aroma."

Under the direction of Stéphanie Bricq, who is of the fourth generation, export sales account for 75% of the production, but much of the cognac is also sold to the more exclusive restaurants (Tour d'Argent, the Ritz, Apicius, Guy Savoy, the Crillon, Oustau de Baumanière, Crocodile) and leading wine and spirits merchants (Fauchon, Legrand, Auge, etc.).

Ragnaud-Sabourin

WINEGROWER-DISTILLER-MERCHANT
LA VOÛTE, AMBLEVILLE (CHARENTE)
1850

This family property, established in the middle of the last century in Grande Champagne, bears the indelible mark of the Gaston Briand (1880-1957). He pioneered the practice of *mise au domaine,* or the bottling of the cognac by the growers and distillers themselves, freeing them from dependency on the great merchant houses. Briand felt that the best lands of the Charente region could produce cognacs of such high quality that blending would not be necessary.

Gaston Briand eventually became the president of the Charente winegrowers association and between the two world wars helped to create the *Bureau national interprofessionel du cognac* (BNIC), which protects the interests of the cognac industry. He also participated in the 1938 commission that revised the official map delimiting the different winegrowing areas, and played a role in the formation of the *Institut national des appellations d'origine* (INAO), whose mission was to protect the producers from counterfeits.

His son-in-law, Marcel Ragnaud, developed the business side of the family interests and oversaw sales and management of over 124 acres of vineyards, planted in ugni blanc, folle blanche, and colombard vines. Paul Sabourin then appeared on the scene when he married Marcel Ragnaud's daughter, giving the business its present name: Ragnaud-Sabourin.

After the succession of two sons-in-law, the estate is presided over today by three women, a rarity in Cognac. They are Denise, the daughter of Gaston Briand and wife of Marcel Ragnaud; her daughter Annie, wife of Paul Sabourin; and her granddaughter Patricia. The "Dames du cognac," as they are sometimes called, have managed to preserve the quality and level of production at the estate, aided by the cellar master, Daniel Dudognon, who learned about cognac thirty years earlier from Marcel Ragnaud. A figure provides an idea of the importance given to the aging of the cognac, an importance to which may be attributed the qualities of these cognacs. The stocks maintained by

Ragnaud-Sabourin represent fifteen times the volume sold annually. A figure of six times is typical of most other houses.

The aging of the brandies always begins in new casks of Limousin oak.

The distillery (above left) and the buildings of the house of Ragnaud-Sabourin (above right).

Ragnaud-Sabourin now sells the following cognacs:

• The Grande Champagne (41% by volume), aged 4 years.

• The VSOP Sélection du Domaine (41%), aged 10 years.

• The Réserve Spéciale (43%), aged 20 years, 10% of which is from folle blanche and colombard grapes.

• Fontvieille (43%), aged 35 years, of which 40% is from folle blanche and colombard grapes.

• Florilège (46%, natural alcohol level), aged 45 years, of which 40% is from folle blanche and colombard grapes.

• Héritage G. Briand Le Paradis (41%), of which 40% is from ugni blanc, 30% from folle blanche and 30% colombard.

An exceptional cognac, 10% from the pre-phylloxera era.

• Héritage Ragnaud (41%), which contains the same proportion of cognacs. Going back to the beginning of the century, its rather woody qualities are complemented by spicier accents.

Since 1996, Grande Champagne, VSOP, Réserve Spéciale, and Fontvieille have been put into a class of their own dubbed "Alliance," each accompanied by a number on the bottle that refers to the age of the cognac (No. 4, No.10, No. 20, No. 35). This approach has the advantage of better informing the consumer without violating the law banning, until a recent date, the attribution of a vintage date to the cognac.

Rémy Martin

WINEGROWER-DISTILLER-MERCHANT
COGNAC (CHARENTE)
1724

At first glance, nothing seems to have set Rémy Martin apart from the rest. It began as a typical Charente winegrowing and distilling establishment, like many that produced cognac in bulk under contract to merchants. Rémy Martin set up shop with another winegrower in the Rouillac region in 1724. But the Martins, among whom many were named Rémy, remained in the shadows of the cognac trade until the late nineteenth century. The Centaure, an original brand, appeared in 1877 but was not officially registered until 1903. In 1904, Paul Rémy Martin, of the sixth generation, took over directing the business, which was at that time at the Château de Lignières and eventually sold to the Ricard group.

Everything changed between 1910 and 1924. The cause of the changes was the arrival of André Renaud, a major winegrower who progressively took over the business and ended up controlling the company's huge stocks of cognac. André Renaud so on saw his opportunity to push Rémy Martin to the top. At the time, the large-scale merchants mainly sold the Trois Étoiles grade of cognac, sometimes along with small portions of better-quality cognac such as XO, Extra, and soon. His idea was to tap into the elitist markets by selling the finer classes of cognac, notably the VSOP and Fine Champagne. This took place in 1927. From 1948 on, Rémy Martin was selling only Fine Champagne, with about fifty percent Grande Champagne. No other class or blend of cognac was commercialized by Rémy Martin.

The goal of this new strategy was to conquer the Asian markets, where an appreciation for the better cognacs had long been overlooked by the merchants.

André Renaud took his advice from a remarkable character by the name of Otto Quien. Quien was half-Dutch and

half-German, born in Shanghai and raised in Switzerland. He had wide experience with the Asian markets, having worked for a major wine and spirits distributor in Indonesia, a company whose business covered the entire Far East. He joined Rémy Martin for good in 1929.

Shrewd businessman that he was, André Renaud managed to set up a vast commercial network throughout the United States and Asia. But he was also an aesthete, and promoted a wonderful coffee-table book on cognac, published in 1962. It was written by Louise de Vilmorin with photographs by Robert Doisneau. As Louise de Vilmorin wrote: "I am only

Quality control at the *chais* of Rémy Martin (above), and a 1935 publicity poster (below).

The stunning success of the Rémy Martin strategy in selling only the VSOP and Fine Champagne did not escape the attention of other merchants. At the end of the 1970s, the "cognac wars," as they were referred to in the media, were raging. The battlefield was the market for Fine Champagne. The term "war" however may seem altogether exaggerated given the subdued and circumspect nature of the good people of Charente.

The response from such giants as Hennessy and Courvoisier, who sold all grades of cognac, and Martell, who specialized in brandies of Borderies origin, was to strike the denomination of Fine Champagne from their catalogues as they no longer considered it worthy of a class of its own. The target of this maneuver was Rémy Martin—whose commercial strategy was based on Fine Champagne. Rémy Martin responded by storming out of the cognac exporter's union, joined by a few other houses. The winegrowers of the two Champagne varieties threw themselves into the fray, outraged that the merchants would wipe out a denomination on which they depended for their livelihood. But respectability prevailed, and peace was soon restored. Rémy Martin won the day, and Fine Champagne was restored to the catalogues of many of the merchants throughout Charente.

RÉMY AND COINTREAU

André Hériard-Dubreuil, attentive to the expansion of the company's cognac sales, organized a worldwide group of wine and spirits distributors, whose main products were the liqueurs of the house of Cointreau and the champagnes of Krug (in 1970), Charles Heidsieck (in 1985), and Piper-Heidsieck (in 1988).

The affair would not go down without a hitch, for the youngest daughter of André Renaud married Max Cointreau, heir to the house of liqueurs. At first, the match enabled Rémy Martin to benefit from Cointreau's international distribution. But Cointreau, only a minor shareholder in the concern, became impatient

following the example set for me by my parents. Their house was always well-kept, and they attached to quality the importance that it deserves. They lived among the most refined connoisseurs, who found in Rémy Martin a cognac that best satisfied their tastes. It increases the spirit of people of spirit; and bestows spirit on those who are in want of it; it adds to the expression a seductive regard and liberates the timid from their sufferings."

André Renaud's son-in-law, André Hériard-Dubreuil, took over in 1965 and continued the relentless expansion of the company during the subsequent twenty-five years. The company became an international colossus, among the four first houses of cognac. The world owes to Rémy Martin the introduction of the green frosted bottle, which has been used to sell VSOP Fine Champagne since 1972. Until then, these models were strictly reserved for bottling the Napoleon class of cognac.

over being left out in the cold when it came to management decisions. Guerrilla warfare broke out in the courts and lasted until 1991 when the group Rémy Martin-Cointreau was finally formed. The union, however begrudging, enabled the house of cognac to stand up to and take on the British and Canadian behemoths that dominated the global market.

André Hériard-Dubreuil extended his activities into the domain of wine. He took control of the Bordeaux brand De Luze and also made acquisitions in Australia, Brazil, China, and California.

A holding company was created in 1990 that included the Scottish group Highland Distillers, sellers of such whiskies as Famous Grouse, Tamdhu, and Highland Park. They represented thirty percent of the concern and it must be acknowleged that today whiskey is indisputably the world's favorite spirit.

Since 1990, the company has been run by Frédérique, André Hériard-Dubreuil's daughter, who is working hard to expand. The company also owns the barrel manufacturer Seguin Moreau, one of the largest in Europe. They make the casks of Limousin oak used exclusively by Rémy Martin for the aging of its cognacs. The company uses its own vineyards and relies on the brandies distilled by more than two thousand growers, bound to Rémy Martin by exclusive contracts beginning in 1965. For the aging of the brandy, Rémy Martin has its own *chais* at Cognac for the more superior products and at Merpins, where the company has built a modern complex for the aging, blending, and bottling of the cognac.

Rémy Martin is everywhere on the French market and has launched numerous

The line offers:
• The VSOP, the foundation of Rémy Martin. The bottle and its label were revised in 1995 to make it more elegant, but the frosted glass was kept.
• The Napoleon Extra Old, also sold in a frosted bottle.
• The XO Spécial, sold in a readily indentifiable rose-styled bottle.
• The Extra Perfection, sold in an elegant carafe.
• The Louis XIII, the jewel of the line and considered for a long time to be one of the most expensive cognacs. It is made only with cognacs of Grande Champagne and is sold in a striking carafe of Baccarat crystal. The carafe is a replica of a sixteenth-century flagon found on the grounds of the battle of Jarnac.

The emblem of the centaur, first introduced by Paul-Émile Rémy Martin at the end of the last century, is found on all of the bottles. He got the idea from his zodiac sign, Sagittarius. He saw in this mythological creature, half-man and half-horse, with its hoofs on the ground and its head raised to the stars, the perfect symbol for publicity campaigns promoting the authenticity of their cognacs: "We can explain everything. Well, almost everything." They also like to promote the impact the cognac has had worldwide: "It's crazy how small the world is getting." In 1994, Rémy Martin made a video that is shown to tourists when visiting the *chais*. Some fifty thousand visitors flock there each year. The video is also used to promote the brand overseas, where ninety-seven percent of its production is exported.

The line of cognacs, all of Fine Champagne origin, is quite obviously modest. No indication of the age of the cognac is given. The most information Rémy Martin is willing to disclose is that "the youngest is a few years older than the minimum allowed age."

cognac. In his mind, the figure illustrated the instinct and vitality of nature combined with the spirit of man—the very essence of cognac.

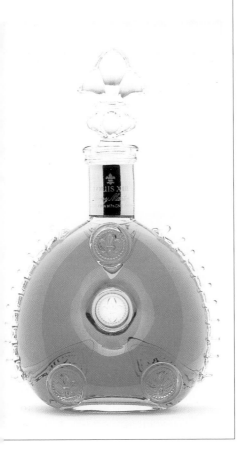

The hooping of a cask is made easier with the use of fire.

Renault

WINEGROWER-DISTILLER-MERCHANT
DOMAINE DE LIGNIÈRES, ROUILLAC
(CHARENTE)
1835

This house, established by Jean-Antoine Renault at Cognac, was one of the pioneers of the practice of shipping in bottles. This is part of the reason for its enormous success on the British and Scandinavian markets at the end of the nineteenth century.

Starting with its main product, the Carte Noire, Renault's development has not met with any major setbacks. In 1963, the company bought another cognac

house, Castillon, founded in 1814. The two families already had close ties dating back to the nineteenth century and for the most part formed by marriage.

Major changes occurred in 1991 when the Pernod-Ricard group, through its subsidiary Bisquit, bought out Castillon-Renault. The company was then transferred from Cognac to Lignières, near Rouillac, where the new managers were headquartered, and where one of the two

CARTE NOIRE
EXTRA

DEPUIS 1835

RENAULT
COGNAC

70 cl   RENAULT - ROUILLAC CHARENTE FRANCE   40 % vol
PRODUCE OF FRANCE

vast *chais* bears the name of Renault. All of its products were suppressed (including the XO) except for two: the Carte Noire Extra and the Carte d'Argent.

The Carte Noire is closer to a Napoleon or an XO and is distinguished by its rather dark color, darker than most old cognacs. The brandies for this cognac are aged up to twenty years and are from the four best areas for growing the grapes. Ten percent of the brandy is made from grapes grown at the Lignière estate, which covers some 494 acres. Once the cognac is blended, it is returned to the cask in order to be aged for a few more months. Smooth and mellow, the Carte Noire is modestly priced, a key factor in its fifth-place ranking in the competition of superior quality cognacs (those cognacs of Napoleon class or better). The principal market for this cognac is Scandinavia, where it accounts for a fourth of all cognac sales. As for the Carte d'Argent, it too is made from brandies which come from the four best growing areas. The brandies are distilled in small stills of 396 gallons. It is aged up to twenty-five years and is allowed to mature for several more years after it is blended. It is sold in a round carafe with a glass, ring-shaped cap.

Roullet

WINEGROWER-DISTILLER-MERCHANT
LE GOULET-DE-FOUSSIGNAC, JARNAC
(CHARENTE)
1780

The Roullet family has been in Foussignac, north of Jarnac, since the eighteenth century. The vineyards are in a Fins Bois area that had once been classified in Champagne. Paul Roullet seems to have gone into the cognac trade some time during the last century, after his marriage to a woman from the Delamain family. At the same time, another family member moved to Paris and opened a cognac shop at the Hôtel Genlis on rue Dauphine.

Opening a shop specializing in cognac was an unusual move for the period. Later, at the beginning of the twentieth century, another family member was named president of the brandy merchant's union.

Today, the company is still in the family's hands, although a while back, a British concern became a major shareholder. Serge Roullet, of the seventh generation, is currently company director.

Amber
Gold

VITICULTEURS   Depuis 1780   DISTILLATEURS

ROULLET
et fils

COGNAC

Mis en bouteille à la propriété

L 22
PRODUCE
OF FRANCE

Roullet et fils
• Le Goulet de Foussignac - France •

FINE COGNAC

The activity of the company is dual. At Foussignac, the brandies that come exclusively from the grapes at the estate are distilled and aged. Two different small stills of 396 and 475 gallons each are used and both are heated by gas. There, the VS Amber Gold (aged 3 to 4 years) and the VSOP (aged 6 to 8 years) are made. The aging of the brandies occurs in rather humid *chais*, partly underground and dating, it is claimed, from the time of Henri IV.

At Cognac, the house of Roullet maintains its other *chais* where a different set of brandies are aged. There, the Napoleon Vieille Réserve, aged about 15 years, and the XO Blue Label are made. Both include cognacs of Grande and Petite Champagne and Fins Bois origins. This is practically the only blend produced by the house of Roullet. Most of the cognacs they sell are made from a single *cru*, often from a single vineyard. They are:

• The Extra Grande Champagne, which comes from the Segonzac region.

• The XO, sold in small carafes.

• The Très Rares, the house's personal treasures, which include the No. 45, which is dry and aromatic—distilled after the World War II; the No. 29, more than 60 years old and characterized by its Borderies origin; and the No. 26, a Grande Champagne, with a natural alcohol content of 41%.

Roussille

WINEGROWER-DISTILLER-MERCHANT
LINARS (CHARENTE)

The Roussille family has been established on its estate at Linars, near Angoulême, for several generations. The estate is located in the Fins Bois area. The house has *chais* for aging the brandy at Cognac.

The house sells a number of classic cognacs under its own name: Trois Étoiles, VSOP, Napoleon Vieille Réserve, and XO.

They also produce several pineaux: the Blanc Vieux, the Rosé, and the Rosé Spécial, which is noted for its excellence.

Louis Royer

MERCHANT
JARNAC (CHARENTE)
1853

When he first started up his business, Louis Royer naturally chose his boyhood

home located by the banks of the Charente at Jarnac. He was only twenty-five years old, but he already had experience as a cellar master from a previous job. He is best remembered as a merchant and winegrower, but he also built a distillery and cooperage. Louis Royer was an avid traveler and he often accompanied his cognacs to their destinations, such as Moscow in 1855 and Philadelphia in 1883.

The house specializes in wholesale, and four generations of the family oversaw the business until 1988, when the Japanese group Suntory took over. A few members of the family decided to remain under the new management, but one, Alain-Louis, preferred to leave and set up his own house of cognac (see Fussigny). The new owners quickly went about expanding production and modernizing the installations. Production from then on focused on four grades of cognac: the VS, the VSOP, the Napoleon, and the XO. All are from Grande and Petite Champagne and Borderies, and the cognacs are sold in glass carafes. With the bee as its mascot, Louis Royer has innovated in terms of promoting its cognacs. Its innovation began at home: the designer Andrée Putman entirely renovated the entrance to

the estate through which visitors must pass. The renovation depicts the whole process involved in making cognac. Lighted globes are mounted on four pillars, each containing a model of a different step in the production process, from a grape vine to a miniature barge of the type once used to transport the casks on the Charente River. In the *chais,* a number of exhibits have been set up for the tourists, each featuring some tool or activity involved in producing cognac.

Since 1994, during the summer months, a dinner has been organized every Friday in La Charmille, the family home of Louis Royer. The soirée is entitled "Discover cognac," and includes a tour of the premises, a cognac sampling exhibit, and finally the dinner, all for a modest sum. A boat rental company on the quay in front of the house offers rides along the Charente. These have become one of the principal publicity tools of the Louis Royer company. They even award a trophy, called the "Great Traveler," in honor of Louis Royer. In 1992, the trophy went to the screenwriter Jean-Claude Carrière. Claude Miserey, president of the French Federation of Men's Clothing Industries, received the coveted trophy in 1994.

Salignac

MERCHANT

JARNAC (CHARENTE)
1809

Probably of Roman origin, the name Salignac is often confused with that of a small town on the banks of the Charente, between Cognac and Saintes. The family line dates as far back as the sixteenth century.

Antoine de Salignac was born in 1753. He went into the cognac trade in partnership with M. Babin in 1802. Seven years later, he assumed sole proprietorship of the small company and was joined by his son Pierre-Antoine. Pierre-Antoine became the director in 1838 and immediately launched a crusade against the major cognac dealers of the period. He was allied with several hundred winegrowers and distillers, who had all become disenchanted with the merchants to whom they sold their products. The alliance, a veritable company in its own right, was an immediate success. Salignac was able to underscore the point that the popularity of cognac was due not to the commercial abilities of the merchants but to the quality of the brandies produced by the growers and distillers.

The name of Salignac quickly became a standard bearer for the different proprietors of the region. This economic alliance soon acquired political significance. Salignac won the support of the landowners, who were conservative and Catholic. They were naturally opposed to the interests of the merchants, who were Protestant and liberal. Chief among their grievances was the merchants' almost exclusive dependence on the British market, including the use of English ships instead of the French merchant marine for transport. As Salignac declared: "For the past several years, brandy has not been selling well on the foreign markets because of poor quality. Their sole merit seems to be due to the brand name on the bottom of the casks. Three houses with this privilege [most likely Hennessy, Martell, and Otard-Dupuy], which had no precedent even under the feudal regime, have gone on to accumulate a fortune, while the humble landowners and producers continue to struggle on the verge of poverty."

This statement is not without its implications—at the time, the peasants of the Charente region were considered to be the best-off economically in France. Salignac was also progressive in his ideas concerning the industry itself. He was one of the first to envision a classification of the many different cognacs in terms of soil and aging. In his struggles against the merchants, he was a staunch advocate of quality.

Portrait of Antoine de Salignac (above), and a poster from an old advertising campaign by the house (below).

"The better the cognac the better the sales. That in turn will have a significant effect on the price of the commodities. If prices on cognac go up with their quality, this will not result in diminishing sales, for it is not the poor who purchase cognac in England. It is a drink exclusively of the rich who care nothing about the price provided they have their pleasure by it." He went on to conclude: "Brandy is your well-being. No other craftsmanship can imitate it; no other land can produce it. Let us then form a pact, an alliance. Let us unite around the holy arch, and the altar of Baal shall be smashed."

The work of Coquand helped to establish the different connections between the land and the brandies it produces.

The descendants of Salignac have continued his work. In 1858, they called upon a geologist, M. Coquand, to study "the physical lay of the land, the geology, paleontology, and mineralogy of the department of Charente." It was the first to examine the link between the different soils and the quality of the cognacs made.

Following the sudden death of Pierre-Antoine de Salignac in 1843, the political polemics that characterized his efforts would end, and the company, headed by his son George until 1864 and later by his other son Louis, would resume the traditional low-key style of the Charente way of doing business.

In 1897, the cooperative company of cognac vineyard owners came under the management of J.-G. Monnet, who eventually would rename the company after himself and transform it into a business. J.-G. Monnet was none other than the father of the famous economist Jean Monnet, an ardent defender of the ideal of a united Europe. He himself worked for several years in the family business at a time when the company was in debt, due to its possesion of stocks of cognac too expensive to sell on the market. The house of Monnet was bought out around 1960 by the German company Scharlachberg.

But the name of Salignac endures. Louis, the son of Pierre-Antoine, started his own company selling cognac in 1898, using the Salignac name and profiting handsomely from its reputation. He would amplify that reputation through an aggressive publicity campaign in a number of foreign countries. Indeed, the cognac was a favorite among such diverse personalities as Winston Churchill, Harry Truman, and Konrad Adenauer.

His nephew, Maurice de Jarnac, followed by his own offspring, kept the business in the family until 1974, when the company was taken over by the Canadian conglomerate Hiram Walker. That company had already purchased Courvoisier ten years earlier. Salignac became a subsidiary of the Jarnac-based company Courvoisier, which was later bought by the British group Allied-Lyons.

Today, the Salignac cognacs include the VS, essentially of Fins Bois origin; the VSOP, largely of Petite and Grande Champagne; the Napoleon; the XO; and the Réserve Très Grande Vieille Fine Champagne, a much more subtle cognac.

Sylène

MERCHANT
LUCHAC, CHASSORS (CHARENTE)
1983

This rather recently established company is notable for the original bottle designs used to sell not just its cognacs but also its other products (armagnac, calvados, whiskey, etc.). The company is situated in a château near Jarnac that once belonged to the nobility. It took its name Sylène (or Silène) from the mythical spirit of the springs and rivers, the foster-father of Dionysus-Bacchus, god of wine.

Its star feature is the Alcotricine, a vessel of pharmaceutical origins, which is available in either large or small sizes and contains a few ounces of cognac. It is sold ten to the box. The box is marked, "A cure for depression."

Sylène also sells the "Test du Connaisseur," or connoisseur's test, which is sort of drinking game that teaches the participant to distinguish between the different varieties of cognac ranging from Trois Étoiles to XO. Next in line is the "The Philosophy Treatise." It is a 12-ounce bottle of cognac, or another spirit sold by the company, that is sold inside a hardback book.

Marquis de Sylène also sells handblown carafes, which contain a cluster of glass grapes, in addition to other specialty bottles.

Testaud

WINEGROWER-DISTILLER-MERCHANT
JARNAC (CHARENTE)

The Testaud family has worked the same land at Barbezieux at the edge of the Champagne and Fins Bois areas for several generations. The family owns four stills, each with a capacity of around 528 gallons. They produce several cognacs ranging from Trois Étoiles to XO. The house specializes in old cognacs, the ages of which are guaranteed, such as the Héritage Grande Fine Champagne or the Réserve Sieur de Plaisance, all of the same *cru*. In 1989, the house was awarded the European Grand Prix de Prestige.

Guy Testaud has also opened a cognac museum on the premises that features the tools of the trade used in the family business, some of which date back several generations.

Tiffon

WINEGROWER-DISTILLER-MERCHANT
JARNAC (CHARENTE)
1875

Méderic Tiffon opened his own cognac company at Jarnac in 1875 after having first been associated with M. Roy during the Second Empire. He focused his activities on the Northern European markets

139

Tiffon owns 99 acres of vineyards in Grande Champagne and Fins Bois, but it still depends on some 350 growers.

and delivered his cognac in casks to the monopolies that controlled the wine and spirits trade in the respective countries.

Since then the company has moved into other markets and of course now sells its cognac in bottles. In 1920, the house bought an elegant *chais* beside the Charente River, where it is headquartered today. It was there in 1936 that the last shipment of cognac in casks was loaded onto a barge for transport to the coast. The barge was aptly named the *France*.

Today, the business is run by the Braastad brothers, Philippe and Antoine, direct descendants of the founder. The company owns ninety-nine acres of vineyards in Grande Champagne and Fins Bois. It purchases the rest of its raw material from some 350 winegrowers. Its two distilleries include seventeen stills, its *chais* contain 15,000 casks holding the equivalent of one million cases of cognac with twelve bottles a case.

Tiffon also bought the house of Boutelleau, which once belonged to the family of the local writer Jacques Chardonne.

Aside from the VS, all cognacs sold by Tiffon are of Fine Champagne origin: the VSOP, Napoleon, XO, Vieux Supérieur, as well as a Grande Champagne. At the Château de Triac, also owned by the house, the Grande Réserve and Vieille Réserve du Château are blended.

The story behind the rise of the house of Trijol is typical of Charente in the careful and methodical striving toward success so characteristic of the people of the region. The company at Saint-Martial-sur-Né has ninety-nine acres of vineyards in Petite Champagne. The house has owned a still since 1859, the year it was registered at the local town hall. In 1954, Maxime Trijol began his activities as a wine and cognac broker. He had sufficiently increased his knowledge of cognac that in 1962 he decided to become a professional distiller.

Today, the company owns eighteen stills, each containing 660 gallons for a total production of 528,000 gallons a year. The family vineyards provide only four percent of the grapes used in production.

Jean-Jacques Trijol, Maxime's son and the present director of the family business, FTD (Famille Trijol-distillateurs), has launched a new line of cognacs named in honor of his father.

The cognacs are made only from grapes from the four first *crus*. The line includes the VS in a Norman bottle, the VSOP in the Flore bottle, the Napoleon (also known as Old Vintage in certain countries) in a Roland bottle, and the XO sold in a carafe. The latter is a remarkable cognac that settles nicely on the palate. Maxime Trijol also has a modern bottling facility, and maintains sizable stocks of old cognac that help to guarantee the quality of its products and to maintain their convenient availability on the market.

THE OTHER PRODUCERS

Despite all the mergers and acquisitions of the last several years, there still are a number of independent producers, whether winegrower-distillers or small companies selling to a select clientele. Below is a list (by no means complete) of some of the producers who, for one reason or another, have caught the attention of connoisseurs and cognac specialists.

Beaulon, in Saint-Dizant-du-Gua (Charente-Maritime): Louis Bigot began distilling brandy at this fifteenth-century château in 1712. The company today is under the supervision of Christian Thomas, who is something of a purist. No additives are allowed in the production of his cognacs. The Grande Fine Extra is remarkable, especially given its Fins Bois origin, where the estate is located.

Bouju, in Segonzac (Charente): Production dates back two centuries and tradition is the hallmark of the company. The brandy is distilled in small stills of 422 gallons and the aging takes place in "red" casks. It should be noted that the company offers a *brut de fût,* a brandy whose natural alcohol content has not been reduced.

Bouron Louis, in Château de la Grange at Saint-Jean-d'Angély (Charente-Maritime): The estate was established in 1832 and includes several different properties and a wonderful stock of cognac. The company is directed by Monique Parias, a descendant of the founders, and her husband, Bernard. It sells several cognacs under its own name and blends the brand Maxim's.

Brugerolle, in Matha (Charente-Maritime).

Collin Jean-Noël, located in Salles-d'Angles (Charente) in Grande Champagne: A distiller-winegrower, noted for the subtlety of his cognacs and their excellent price-quality ratios.

Cosson Gilles, in Guimps (Charente): The family has worked the same 124 acres for six generations. They distill and age cognacs from Grande Champagne only, ranging from VSOP to the Très Vieux, and produce a few pineaux as well.

Couprié, in Ambleville (Charente): A family of growers and distillers who own a vineyard of fifty-four acres in Grande Champagne.

Estève Jacques, in Celles (Charente-Maritime): A family business for several generations in Petite Champagne. They offer cognacs of a very high quality.

Fine Goule, in Archiac (Charente-Maritime): This is a partnership between two winegrowing families in one of the best parts of Petite Champagne.

Gaston de Lagrange, in Cognac (Charente): This commercial brand was introduced by the Martini & Rossi group in the 1970s, intended for mass distribution. It uses the complete title of the barons of Otard de la Grange as its brand name, the brand Otard being the principal product sold by the group. It rapidly became one of the ten best-selling cognacs in France, and is exported to fifty different countries. The line includes a VSOP, a Napoleon, and an XO of Grande Champagne aged thirty years.

Giraud, in Châteauneuf (Charente): The family has lived in the Grande Champagne area since 1650 and has been distilling brandy since 1837. Paul Giraud and his son Paul-Jean, presently in charge of the operation, emphasize the soil's characteristics in their cognacs, and they never add sugar or caramel. The line offers a VSOP, aged six years, Napoleon, and Vieille Réserve.

Gourry de Chadeville, in Segonzac (Charente): The family has been on this property since 1619. It distills and ages only Grande Champagne cognacs, from a VSOP to a Très Vieux, along with several pineaux.

Grateaux Maurice, in Chérac (Charente-Maritime): This is a rare example of a house that specializes only in cognacs of Borderies origin, famous for its particular floral characteristics.

Grönstedts is a Swedish cognac, elaborated from distilled wine from Cognac since 1846. It is aged in oak casks from Limousin and is sold as Trois Étoiles (seven or eight years), VO, XO, and Extra, which is aged twenty or twenty-two years.

Guerbé, in Juillac-le-Coq (Charente): The house sells cognacs that are distilled and aged on the premises. The vineyards cover eighty-four acres in Grande Champagne.

Lafite Rothschild, in Pauillac: The Rothschild properties have lent their name to a collection of very interesting cognacs, largely of Borderies origin.

Landier Rémi, in Foussignac (Charente): Winegrower-distiller producing some superb cognacs of Fins Bois origin.

Leteux Jacques, in Blanzac-les-Matha (Charente-Maritime): This winegrower-distiller has been around forever. They sell several pineaux and a few cognacs (VO, VSOP, XO).

Logis de la Montagne, in Challignac (Charente): The property in the Fins Bois area has been cultivated by the family for four generations. The current director is M. Bonnin.

Monnet, in Cognac (Charente): This merchant company was founded as an offshoot of the company created by the Marquis de Salignac. The company bears the stamp of Jean Monnet, father of European unity. It is under German ownership today.

Mounié Denis, in Jarnac (Charente): The company was founded in 1838 and had its moment of glory as the official supplier to King Edward VII. It was later bought by Bénédictine and then Hine.

Planat, in Cognac (Charente): A merchandising firm founded in 1828 by Charles-Abel Planat de la Faye, who was deputy mayor of the town. One of the town's boulevards bears his name.

Prunier, in Cognac (Charente): This old house of cognac, founded at the beginning of the seventeenth century, has always belonged to the same family. The Réserve is an excellent cognac, aged twenty years.

Robin Jules: This old and mighty house of cognac collapsed following the war due to the loss of the Chinese market—its main source of revenue. The house was then bought by Martell.

Rouyer Guillet, in Saintes (Charente): One of the few houses focusing on sales that is located at Saintes. It was founded at the beginning of the eighteenth century by Philippe Guillet and has remained in the same family ever since.

Roy René, in Juillac-le-Coq (Charente): Winegrower-distiller on seventy-four acres in Grande Champagne.

THE COGNATHEQUE, A COGNAC BOUTIQUE

The boutique, La Cognatheque, in the center of Cognac two steps from the place François-1er, has the best display of cognac in the world, and the only one in the region. More than 250 different brands are sold here, not including the pineaux des Charentes and other cognac-based liqueurs. The entire line covers cognacs ranging from the Trois Étoiles class to others that cost more than 3,000 francs a bottle.

Surprisingly, it is not a local Charente citizen who came up with this brilliant idea. When he first arrived in Charente, Serge Arrou was astonished to find that no one in the most famous brandy-producing region in the world had ever thought of opening up such a store. From Cognac to Jarnac, each house had for a long time welcomed visitors. The larger companies even employ their own guides, have their own historical and production exhibits, and of course offer their own cognac-tasting sessions.

Nevertheless, before the Cognatheque, no establishment existed where the cognac lover or tourist could appreciate the stylistic variety of the many cognacs currently available.

"Being independent of any authority," says Serge Arrou, "we take only those products that we consider worthy of the appellation." The role of the Cognatheque, in addition to selling cognac, is to assist and inform the clients. "Aside from a select clientele—often of foreign origin—who know what they want, we consider it our role in most cases to suggest a brand suitable to the client's tastes. If we make the effort to help the customer, French or otherwise, that's proof enough of the vitality of the market here in France, which is contrary to the prevailing opinion." Mail-order sales, notably for hard-to-obtain cognacs, have become another major activity of the Cognatheque.

After fifteen years in business, Serge Arrou has formed definite ideas about cognac and the process by which it is made. Thus, he deplores the confusion surrounding the quality of the XO class, which has all too often been underestimated, in his opinion. He is also adamantly opposed to the idea of marketing cognac as a mixer. "Cognac is pure quintessence, and any dilution is an abomination." He is also on guard against the mounting influence of foreign brandies, some of which rival in quality the Trois Étoiles cognacs.

Serge Arrou's dream is to establish other Cognatheques in Paris and other cities such as London and New York. He imagines a place similar to the one he has in Cognac, with armchairs and an area reserved for cigar smokers. Cognac, it must be acknowledged, could do with these sorts of establishments, which provide the public with an experience that will convince them of the superiority of cognac over other spirits.

La Cognatheque, 8 place Jean-Monnet, 16100 Cognac. Telephone: 05 45 82 43 31.

The Cognatheque owned by Serge Arrou has the best display of cognac anywhere.

The pineau des Charentes

Pineau des Charentes is made with cognac and fresh juice from ripened grapes. It belongs to a category of wine liqueurs, and the pineau is perhaps the best and most famous representative. Legend in Charente has it that pineau des Charentes was invented when a winegrower unwittingly poured grape juice into a cask containing a small amount of cognac. He then left it for a few months and forgot about it. One day he came across the cask by chance, tasted its contents and was delighted with his discovery.

In fact, wine-based liqueurs are an old tradition in many winegrowing regions throughout France and elsewhere. Their origins are not clear historically. All that is known is that the practice of conserving a volume of grape juice after each harvest and mixing it with brandy has existed for quite a long time. The purpose of mixing brandy with the grape juice is to prevent its fermentation. The result is a dessert drink that goes well with a fruit dessert or a tarte.

The pineaux are very similar to fortified wines, such as port. There is one important difference, however. For wines such as port, the brandy is added after the wine is fermented (or as it is fermenting) and not before. That qualifies them as wines in their own right. For a pineau, it is the taste of the grape juice and its sweetness that is important, while the brandy serves mainly to preserve those qualities and enhance its aroma.

THE STRICT CONDITIONS FOR MAKING PINEAU DES CHARENTES

For a long time, pineau was a private affair, reserved for consumption by the local winegrowers and inhabitants of the region. In contrast to cognac, this beverage was not commercialized until much later, and somewhat hesitantly, during the interwar period. It is above all a product of the smaller independent cognac producers, the larger companies having considered it to be of only limited appeal. A law dated July 6, 1935, conferred upon pineau des Charentes its commercial status, which was protected again by law in 1945 with the official *appellation d'origine controlée* (AOC). It is also one of the rare products requiring two AOC elements, with the cognac being likewise registered before being added to the blend.

According to the present legal description of a pineau, it is obtained by blending three-quarters grape juice and one-quarter cognac in an oak barrel. These two components must have the same origins.

The grapes must be of just the right age. This ensures that the grapes are at their juiciest. The juice must contain six ounces of sugar per liter, or ten percent by volume. The cognac is added immediately after the grapes are pressed to prevent any fermentation, and the cognac must be aged at least one year before it is mixed with the juice. The final product must have an alcohol content between sixteen and twenty-two percent by volume, and production must not exceed 30 hectoliters (79.2 gallons) for each hectare (2.47 acres) of harvested grapes.

Finally, to qualify as a pineau, the blend must be aged at least one year in an oak cask and possess a sugar content of 4.5 to 5 ounces per liter.

Moreover, the name "pineau des Charentes" is only attributed after it has been tasted by specialists who are members of the *Institut national des appellations d'origine*. The job is to guarantee that the quality of the product is up to standard. Following filtration, the bottling of the pineau must occur at its place of origin.

At this point, many of the more common pineaux are ready for market. However, a number of others will continue to age for a longer time in their oak casks. To qualify as "vieux," it must be aged five years, and to qualify as "extra-vieux," it must be aged at least ten years; and these pineaux must undergo an additional

control before they are put on the market. They are of the highest quality and have a wonderful effect on the palate. However, their production is limited.

There are two main types of pineau: the blanc, or white, and the rosé, sometimes called red. The pineau blanc is made from the same grapes used to produce cognac: the ugni blanc, folle blanche, colombard, as well as other varieties such as the sémillion, the sauvignon, and the montils.

The pineau rosé, fruitier than the blanc, is made from cabernet sauvignon grapes or cabernet franc, malbec and merlot, which the winegrowers of Charente cultivate to make table wine.

The total production of pineau des Charentes has grown over the years and currently stands at 2.1 to 2.6 million gallons per year, and even in excess of 3.1 million gallons for some years. France is the main consumer of pineau and accounts for three-quarters of all sales. The other quarter is exported mainly to francophone countries such as Belgium and Quebec, with the remainder being consumed by Northern European countries. Right now, it is not worth the trouble to market the product even as a cognac derivative on markets in the United States or Asia.

Sales also vary with the seasons, and are naturally highest during the summer months, as tourists to Charente are major clients of the local pineau trade that flourishes among the smaller producers.

The small producers, who account for the majority of pineau production, benefit from legislation that dictates that the grape juice and cognac must come from

the same property. Otherwise, the product does not qualify as an AOC and cannot be sold. For the major merchants, this poses a serious problem since most of the goods they procure come from many different wine growers and distillers, and it is not worth maintaining stocks of cognac for the sole purpose of making a pineau.

As a result, very few of the existing brands of pineau have ever managed to impose themselves on the market. This is mainly because the small producers do not have at their disposal the impressive distribution network used by the more commercial houses. Only the cooperatives have managed to get their products to market on a large scale. That is the case of Unicoop, which sells Reynac on the mass market at a volume of 422,400 to 475,200 gallons a year. Another example is the Château de Didonne, which belongs to the cooperative Cozes-Saujon. They sell four different brands: Marquis de Didonne, Monsieur de Didonne, Maine Gansac, and Fontgalant. Nevertheless, most of the brands are sold directly on the producer's premises.

TASTING AND PROMOTING

A pineau des Charentes is to be served at the same temperature as the aging *chais,* which is to say about 54 degrees Fahrenheit. Today, the trend is to drink it frappé, or 42 degrees. It is important to avoid adding ice as this ruins the aromatic qualities of the drink.

Though it is an aperitif, the pineau is often enjoyed as a cocktail, as a dessert

substitute, or even accompanying certain dishes such as foie gras, melon, and fish.

The appeal of the pineau is beginning to be appreciated outside of France. In 1994, during a blind taste test at the International Wine and Spirit Competition, the pineau blanc Château Paulet won a silver medal. The promotion of pineau des Charentes did not begin in force until 1948, when the Duke and Duchess de La Rochefoucauld decided to enhance its standing. To that effect, they organized promotional events at their château in Charente and went on to create an association called the *Principauté du franc pineau.*

In 1950, this organization became the *Confrérie du franc pineau.* Its members wear a large red cape, a large hat, and a pewter necklace. This fraternity had the happy effect of bringing together people of many different backgrounds in a promotional ploy to popularize pineau des Charentes.

Tasting and mixing

The prevailing view of cognac in France is that it is a brandy to be enjoyed only as an after-dinner digestif served undiluted. However, in both historical and geographical terms, this notion is completely false.

In fact, for a long time cognac was consumed in France at any time during the day, usually served as a cordial. Until World War II, it was sold in cafés and brasseries as a *fine à l'eau,* which is to say, mixed with fresh water or soda water.

Only the very best cognacs were reserved for after-dinner enjoyment, as a dignified and proper way of concluding a fine meal.

Cognac "slipped on the ice cube," as they say in France, and lost out to other brandies and spirits, notably whiskey, which had gained widespread popularity as a spirit that went well with ice. Luckily for the merchants and growers of Charente, other consumers outside of France have not restricted their cognac consumption to after dinner. In the Far East, for example, it is common to drink cognac diluted with water throughout the entire meal.

Fifty years after whiskey, cognac has finally played the aperitif card.

Some three-fourths of the cognac consumed by the French is of the Trois Étoiles class. They appear to be largely indifferent to the better grades of cognac, which account for over fifty percent of exports. This is not to say they have lost all interest in the finer cognacs, but they would be well advised to rediscover the aromatic richness and diversity of their national product, and learn to appreciate it as much as it is appreciated elsewhere.

In Japan and throughout the Far East, it is customary to have a bottle of VSOP or XO in one's bar as a sign of class, and to offer a guest a snifter is a gesture that is warmly appreciated.

The BNIP, along with the merchants, have for several years attempted to redress this lack of interest among the French and to reinstill a taste for cognac. Dubbed operation "Cognac VO" (for "original version"), the campaign has promoted cognac as a cocktail drink to be enjoyed with soda water, tonic, or ice.

Several houses have also embarked upon a vigorous promotional strategy in France in order to reconquer a market that has been largely ignored in favor of the export market.

The wood brings mellowness, balance, and roundness.

Thus, Hennessy organizes promotional events in cafés and discotheques to kindle interest in Hennessy Glace, for which a special glass was created. Rémy Martin, on the other hand, proposes miniature bottles of cognac to accompany coffee. However, legal obstacles, such as the Evin law in France, impose limits on the extent to which publicity can be used when it comes to selling alcoholic drinks.

THE ART OF TASTING COGNAC

Another false notion entertained by the French is that cognac is best served in a large snifter, the size of which can sometimes rival the dimensions of a fish bowl. In fact, these glasses are among the worst to use for drinking cognac. The round shape traps the aromas emanating from the cognac and prevents them from adequately reaching the nose of the imbiber.

The vessel most appropriate for cognac is the tulip-shaped glass, which has a relatively wide rim and an enlarged round base, which is the right shape to retain and concentrate the aromas. This was the traditional cognac glass until it was re-

placed in the early twentieth century by the balloon-shaped snifter. However, it is still used by the cellar masters (*maîtres de chai*) when sampling the cognac. An interesting variation of the tulip glass has been developed by Cristal d'Arques for its "Oenologues" series. It was developed in consultation with several cellar masters under the direction of Alain Royer (A. Fussigny cognacs). This glass, with a somewhat unusual height for its type, more effectively concentrates the aromas for a better and more satisfying enjoyment.

Just over half an ounce of cognac is enough to fully experience its qualities. Tasting cognac, whether it be fresh from the still or a very old product, is above all an experience of the nose. Certainly the eye will be pleased by the clarity of the liquid in the glass and will delight in the nuanced colors that range from golden yellow to the more sensuous dark brown as they pass through a spectrum of ochers and ambers. But it is the nose that ultimately decides the true quality of a cognac. The satisfying way the brandy settles on the tongue and the effect of the alcohol are less important. Indeed, the alcohol has the effect of dispersing the different aromas as they mix over the palate.

A famous saying of Talleyrand's captures the idea. To a German ambassador who had just swallowed a glass of cognac in one gulp, Talleyrand remarked: "That is not the way to drink cognac. Take the glass in the palm of your hand. Warm it and swirl it in the glass until the liquor exhales its aroma. Then, hold it to your nose and breathe in." "And then, monseigneur?" the ambassador asked. "Then, monsieur, put the glass down and let's discuss the experience."

Obviously, Talleyrand did not intend to be as masochistic as to suggest that a great cognac is only to be discussed and not to be consumed. However, the point is well made. It takes time to sensitize the olfactory organs. Because of its aromatic complexity, a great brandy requires a bit of time to express each of its individual aromas. Often five or even ten minutes should elapse before the cognac is ready to be tasted.

Although there is an advantage in slowly airing the cognac by swirling it in its glass, it serves no purpose whatsoever to warm the cognac in the palm of the hand. Once the cognac reaches 86 degrees Fahrenheit, the stronger constituents escape too rapidly to the detriment of a balanced release of the more subtle aromas. It can also help

The shape of the glass is not
as irrelevant as one would think
when it comes to fully appreciating
a cognac. The aroma, even more than
the taste, is the important quality by
which to judge the cognac. The role of the
glass is to concentrate the aromas for the
olfactory organs that make up the nose. A glass
with a large base and relatively circumscribed
rim is considered by the experts to have the ideal
shape. Accordingly, the form most favored will
resemble the shape of a large winter pear, with
the upper part cut off. Another excellent form
favored by connoisseurs is the tulip-shaped
glass, which resembles a young tulip on a
clear spring morning as it is just opening
its petals. Finally, there is the
egg-shaped glass, if
you can picture
your soft-
boiled
break-
f a s t
e g g
s i t -
t i n g
on its pe-
destal and
ready to eat. But
what good are these
analogies? The tulip, the pear,
and the egg are as much a part of good living as is cognac.

The cognac tasting glass, according to a text that appeared in 1870, and reproduced in the *Livre du cognac* by Bruno Sepulchre.

to add a bit of pure water. The water helps to attenuate the strength of the alcohol, which can suppress some of the aromas. A little water in fact helps to enhance the more subtle constituents.

It is not at all easy to distinguish between the different aromas that can be found in the many types of cognac. But that is perhaps the joy to be had in discovering a new sensation when trying for the first time an unknown cognac. Every step of a cognac's production acts in concert with the others in assuring the uniqueness of the end result, from the soil, to the distillation, the aging and finally to the blending. All the same, it is possible to more or less identify a cognac according to its principal aromas, especially with respect to the different *crus*.

Grande Champagne: it is known for its subtlety, distinction, and the persistence of its odor. The aromas are divided into two categories: the first is above all floral in character, with an accent of flowers of the vine, of dry lime, and vine shoots. The other aromas are softer, somewhat wine accented, and distinguished by a very discreet odor of alcohol.

Petite Champagne: the analogies to Grande Champagne are apt, but the aromatic persistence is less, and the quality is not as subtle. On the other hand, the fruitiness is more developed in Petite Champagne. The Petite Champagne, from the area around Archiac, is noted for being lighter than the other cognacs of this *cru*.

Borderies: the smallest definable area of cognac is characterized best by a dominant floral aroma, while the fruitier aromas are much more discreet, if not altogether absent. The floral aroma has a hint of iris and lilac in it. The Borderies are less complex aromatically than the Champagnes, but their aromatic persistence is just as satisfying.

Bois: the quality of the cognacs decreases from Fins Bois to Bois Ordinaires. Floral aromas are weak if not completely absent, while the fruitier aromas are more pronounced. The brandies are generally heavier, lacking in complexity, and characterized by an "earthy flavor" that is rather musky, a sign of poor quality. A good distiller can suppress these faults by intensifying the alcohol reduction.

Aside from the soil from which it comes, other factors contribute to the personality of a cognac. The most important factor is of course the aging, from which the cognac derives its mellow tone, its balance, and its fullness. It is also at this stage that it acquires the vanilla nuances that supplement its aromatic complexity. The unique overripe flavor called *rancio* appears after about ten years of aging in the casks. It is a unique candied aroma resembling the odor of balsam.

It shouldn't be forgotten that cognac can be an agreeable ingredient in certain dishes. Flaming, be it of lobster or crêpes, is its best known culinary role. Still, cognac is an important ingredient in any number of sauces that are either cold, such as in vinaigrette or mayonnaise, or warm, with crème fraîche. Not to be overlooked is the important role cognac plays in a variety of desserts, such as chocolate mousse or bavarian cream, where it works to marvelous effect.

Finally, cognac is an excellent mixer and the main ingredient of a number of cocktails. In a mixer, the Trois Étoiles is better to use, and anything superior to a VSOP would be a waste. This is because the exquisite aromatic qualities of the finer cognacs are immediately lost upon contact with the other ingredients in the cocktail.

The glass developed by Cristal d'Arques (above) is slightly different from the tulip glass (below).

Cognac and cocktails

Vanderbilt

Short drink, served at any time. Pour into a shaker:
- equal parts cognac and cherry brand
- two dashes of cane sugar syrup
- two dashes of angostura

Stir with a spoon and serve in a cocktail glass. Add a maraschino cherry.

Side Car

Pour into a shaker half full of ice:
- one part lemon juice
- three parts Cointreau
- six parts cognac

Shake well and pour into a chilled cocktail glass. This classic dry cocktail was invented in 1933 at Harry's Bar in Paris.

American Rose

Pour into a shaker that is half full of ice:
- 1 jigger of cognac
- dash of Pernod
- dash of grenadine
- 1/2 ripe peach

Shake for a while and pour into a champagne flute containing a bit of ice. Top off with champagne. Add a maraschino cherry. This relaxing drink develops some rather complex aromas.

Horse's Neck

Place a long twist of lemon rind in a tumbler. Add ice and pour in 1 jigger of cognac and a dash of angostura. Fill the glass with gingerale and serve with a straw. This dry refreshing drink is perfect for hot weather.

Brandy Eggnog

Pour into a shaker half full of ice:
- 1 spoonful of powdered sugar
- 1 egg yolk
- 4/10 cognac
- 6/10 fresh milk

Shake well and pour into a glass tumbler. Sprinkle with grated nutmeg. Very refreshing, this long drink can also be served hot. Served cold it is very thirst-quenching.

Calimero

A short drink to be served at any time of the day.
Pour into a shaker half full of ice:
- 3/10 cognac
- 1 part Grand Marnier
- 1 part coffee liqueur
- 3 parts orange juice
- 1 part lemon juice
- 1 part egg white

Shake vigorously and pour into a small tumbler. Decorate with an orange slice.

Kriss

Into a mixing glass with ice pour:
- 4 parts cognac
- 2 parts white vermouth
- 1 part lemon juice
- 2 parts Amaretto di Saronno
- a dash of sugar

Stir with a spoon and pour into a large tumbler. Fill up with tonic water. Decorate with a lemon slice. This strong long drink is also exquisitely thirst-quenching.

Kriss and Brandy Sour.

Hercule

A long drink that can be served at any time. Pour into a large tumbler with a few ice cubes:
- 2 parts cognac
- 2 parts Amaretto di Saronno
- 1 part grenadine
- 5 parts orange juice

Stir well and decorate with an orange slice.

Three Miller

A short drink and aperitif. Pour into a shaker half filled with ice:
- 5 parts cognac
- 3 parts white rum
- 1 part grenadine
- 1 part lemon juice

Shake and pour into a cocktail glass.

Alexander's Sister

A short drink and best served after dinner. Pour into a shaker half filled with ice:
- 4 parts cognac
- 3 parts coffee liqueur
- 3 parts crème fraîche

Shake and pour into a cocktail glass. Sprinkle with grated nutmeg.

American Beauty

A short drink that can be served at any time:
Pour into a shaker half filled with ice:
- 2 parts cognac
- 2 parts dry vermouth
- 2 parts freshly squeezed orange juice
- 2 parts grenadine
- 2 parts clear crème de menthe

Shake and pour into a cognac snifter. Gently pour a small amount of red port so that it remains on the surface.

Morning Glory

A long drink and aperitif. Pour into a shaker half filled with ice:
- 4 parts cognac
- 3 parts Cointreau or Triple Sec
- 3 parts orange juice
- 2 dashes of angostura
- 2 dashes of pastis
- 1 teaspoon of powdered sugar

Shake and pour into a large tumbler. Fill with soda water and decorate with a lemon slice.

Brandy Sour

Pour into a shaker half filled with ice:
- 7 parts cognac
- 3 parts lemon juice
- a dash of sugar

Shake and pour into a small tumbler and decorate with a lemon slice. This drink is best when served before a meal, as the blend of cognac and lemon juice stimulates the appetite.

Stinger

Pour into a shaker half filled with ice:
- 3 parts clear crème de menthe
- 7 parts cognac

Shake and pour into a cocktail glass. This mild cocktail is best served before a meal. Using green crème de menthe (peppermint) makes the drink an Emerald.

Glossary

Acquit "jaune d'or"

The fiscal and economic transport permit that guarantees the conditions according to which the cognac is made. It legally attests the right to use the cognac appellation.

Aire de production

Production area: Designates the geographic zone in which a vineyard qualifies for a given *appellation d'origine*. For cognac, the decree of May 1, 1909, set the boundaries of the Charente cognac-producing region. The decree of January 13, 1938, established the list of communes entitled to the sub-regional appellations (see "Cru").

Alambic

Still: The device used to distill brandies. It is made of three main parts: the *chaudière*—boiler or pot; the *chapiteau*—head, including the swan's neck pipe; and the *réfrigérent*—condenser, or water jacket, including the serpentine pipe. Double distilling is used in making cognac, and the Charente still is required to be made of copper and to be heated by an open fire. According to the decree of December 14, 1977, its capacity cannot exceed 792 gallons, which limits the volume of wine to 660 gallons.

Alcool pur

Pure alcohol, also called ethyl alcohol or absolute alcohol—one hundred percent alcohol by volume. It is measured in hectoliters (26.4 gallons) at 68 degrees Fahrenheit. It is used as a standard for assessing production and sales statistics.

Assemblage

Blending: The mixing of cognacs of different ages and production areas. It is done in order to obtain a more balanced and consistent product. It also enables the producer or seller to achieve a distinctive style. Almost all cognacs sold on the market are blends.

Bonne chauffe

The second distillation that yields a brandy not exceeding seventy-two percent alcohol by volume.

Bouilleur

A brandy distiller. Three different categories are recognized in Charente: the *bouilleur de cru,* who distills his own production for the distillery's own needs or on contract for other producers; the *bouilleur de profession,* who works for a cognac merchant on the firm's premises distilling wine purchased from growers; and the cooperative, which distills wine provided by its members.

Brandy

According to European regulations, brandy refers to any alcohol distilled from wine, whether blended with other wine distillates or not. The distillate must be aged at least one year in an oak container (or six months if the volume is less than one hectoliter, or 26.4 gallons). The content of volatile substances must not exceed 125 grams (4.5 ounces) per hectoliter of pure alcohol. The methanol content must not exceed 200 grams (7.1 ounces) per hectoliter of pure alcohol. The minimum alcohol content must not be less than thirty-six percent by volume. Brandy includes a number of products that do not conform to the specifications of cognac, such as an origin in the Charente region. In English-speaking countries, the term brandy is often misused as a synonym for cognac.

A tasting in a Hennessy *chai*.

Brouillis

The product of the first distillation, with twenty-seven and thirty-two percent alcohol by volume.

Caisse

Case: The commercial unit corresponding to twelve standard 24-ounce bottles of cognac with an alcohol level of forty percent. The total content of a case is 8.4 liters (8.9 quarts) with a total alcohol content corresponding to 3.36 liters (3.6 quarts) of pure alcohol.

Campagne de distillation

In Charente, this is the period between the harvest and the following March 31. The end of the official period of distillation sets the date from which the brandy's age is marked. Recently distilled brandies are counted as zero years old and must be aged at least one year. It is illegal to distill alcohol in the region after March 31 and until the end of the next grape harvest.

Campagne viticole

The period beginning September 1 and ending August 31 the following year.

The height of the vine is a distinctive mark of the plants used in making cognac.

Cépages

Vine type: Three principal types of vine and five secondary ones are authorized for the grapes used in making cognac. The most extensively planted by far is the ugni blanc. To a much lesser extent, the colombard and the folle blanche are also used.

Chai jaune d'or

A storage structure where only cognac is kept and aged. It is by law not to be used for any other alcohol.

Chauffe-vin (réchauffe-vin)

An accessory used on some stills in which the reservoir of white wine is traversed by a column exiting from the boiler. It is used to economize on energy by heating the wine before it is distilled.

Cognac

The *appellation controlée,* or official title, limited to brandy distilled and aged according to strict conditions. It must be distilled in the Charente region from white wine made from grapes grown in Charente. The legal statutes specify the winegrowing area, the different varieties of grape permitted, the methods of vinification and distillation, and the rules for storage, aging and merchandising.

Cru

In Charente, the term designates a sub-region corresponding to a given type of cognac. There are six *crus:* Grande and Petite Champagne, Borderies, Fins Bois, Bons Bois, and Bois Ordinaires (also called Bois communs or Bois à terroir).

Esprit

Esprit de vin formerly designated the alcohol from the second distillation. Today, it refers to the product of the third Charente distillation and contains eighty to eighty-five percent alcohol by volume. It is used only to prepare the *liqueur d'expédition* for champagnes and other sparkling wines.

Fine

According to French regulations, this term refers to a superior quality of distillate, with an *appellation d'origine controlée,* or legally registered name. It is used above all for cognac and calvados. The term Fine Champagne refers to a blend of cognacs from Grande and Petite Champagne, with at least fifty percent of the blend being Grande Champagne.

Fût

Cask: According to regulations, the wood used in making the casks for aging cognac must be oak from the forests of either Limousin or Tronçais. Their capacity must be between 80 and 105 gallons.

Gabare

A flat-bottomed boat used until World War II to transport cognac on the Charente River.

Napoleon

A class of cognac that has been aged for a duration longer than a VSOP but shorter than a XO. There is no fixed legal definition.

Paradis

A special *chai* or warehouse, often locked and protected, where the oldest cognacs of a producer or merchant are stored.

Part des anges

The Angel's Share: The percentage of cognac (between 2.5 to 3 percent per year) that evaporates during the aging process.

Petites eaux

Term for the mixture of distilled water and brandy used in reducing the alcohol content of a cognac before it is sold. Its use is preferable to water alone for preserving the cognac's qualities.

Phylloxera

The insect, or vine louse, that devastated the vineyards of Charente from 1870 on. The vineyards were restored by replanting with grafted vines.

Pressoir

The use of a continuous press (Archimedes' screw) is forbidden in the cognac-producing region.

Serpentin

The spiral tube that is used to trap, cool, and condense the vapors leaving the still.

Sucrage

A technique, also called chaptalization, that consists of adding sugar to the fermenting wine. It is forbidden in Charente.

Têtes

The first brandies yielded at the beginning of the distillation. They are discarded.

Torula compniacensis richon

A mold that thrives on the vapors emitted by the aging brandy. It blackens the walls and ceilings of the *chais* where the cognac is being aged or stored.

Trois Étoiles

Three Star: The youngest grade of cognac (aged less than four and a half years). It is more and more frequently called VS (Very Superior).

Vins vinés

Wine reinforced with brandy to an alcohol content of between eighteen and twenty-four percent. It is exported to Germany for the most part, where it is distilled for making Weinbrand.

VSOP

Initials of an English term (Very Superior Old Pale) designating a class of cognac that has been aged between four and a half and six and a half years.

XO

Initials of an English term (Extra Old) designating a class of cognac that has been aged for more than six and a half years.

(Principal source: "Le Cognac, conseil économique et social régional de Poitou-Charentes," June 1993)

Walls of the *paradis chai* at Dor blackened by the fungus *Torula compniacensis richon*, which thrives on brandy vapors.

Statistics

THE VINEYARDS

In 1992, the 204,113 acres of vines devoted to the production of white wine used in making cognac comprised 13,974 vineyards. In the early 1870s, before the spread of phylloxera, the vines covered more than 691,60 acres.

THE HARVEST

In 1992, 306.2 million gallons of distillable white wine were produced, which amounted to 24.6 million gallons of pure alcohol. In the 1950s, the harvest for making white wine represented only 39.6 to 79.2 million gallons.

EMPLOYMENT

The entire cognac industry employs 30,000 individuals, of whom 20,000 work in the winegrowing sector, 5,500 work in distilling and sales, and 4,500 in various related functions (bottling, boxing, barrel making, etc.)

COST

In August 1995, a bottle of Trois Étoiles cognac sold for 110 French francs, of which the state took 50.03 francs, or 45 percent. This represents commercial duties (25.37 francs), taxes for Social Security (5.88 francs) and VAT (18.78 francs). The remainder broke down as follows: 19.99 francs for distribution costs, 12.04 francs for the wine, 2 francs for the distillation, 25.95 for the aging, packaging, advertising, transport, and the retail profit margin. Another increase in commercial duties occurred on January 1, 1997.

SALES (1995 figures)

94.4 percent of the total cognac production is exported, half of that being superior cognacs (anything better than Trois Étoiles), representing 10.2 billion francs. Cognac is the second-ranking French wine or spirits exports.

THE MARKETS (1995 figures)

The French market is the seventh-largest cognac market in the world and accounts for 6.9 million bottles sold, or 5.5 percent of the world market.

Cognac is sold in 170 different countries. Sales in 1980 reached 17.7 million bottles and have not increased since, largely because of dropping rates of consumption and the increasing duties imposed on spirits, which have increased tenfold in thirty years.

DISTRIBUTION OF EXPORTS WORLDWIDE

Europe: 33.6 percent of the volume and 21.7 percent of revenues.
America: 22.7 percent of the volume and 17.1 percent of revenues.
Asia: 42.9 percent of the volume and 59.7 percent of revenues.

PRINCIPAL IMPORTERS

United States: 1.96 million cases, or 1.44 billion francs.
Hong Kong: 1.25 million cases, or 2.26 billion francs.
United Kingdom: 978,228 cases, or 673.74 million francs.
Japan: 913,945 cases, or 1.21 billion francs.
Singapore: 656,093 cases, or 966.45 million francs.
Germany: 482,806 cases, or 366.62 million francs.
Malaysia: 276,485 cases, or 396.29 million francs.
Taiwan: 270,128 cases, or 604.42 million francs.
Ireland: 191,766 cases, or 117.78 million francs.
Belgium-Luxembourg: 190,891 cases, or 154.93 million francs.
Netherlands: 149,620 cases, or 111.85 million francs.
Denmark: 130,372 cases, or 114.78 francs.
Finland: 117,903 cases, or 106.44 million francs.
Italy: 108,415 cases, or 81.48 million francs.

ACKNOWLEDGEMENTS

The author is indebted to those cognac merchants and producers who provided him with the information essential to the writing of this book, and would also like to thank the *Bureau National Interprofessionel du Cognac* and in particular Claire Coates, director of public relations, and the *Comité National du Pineau des Charentes*.

PHOTOGRAPHY

All of the photographs of bottles and cocktails are by Matthieu Prier.
All other photographs are by Jean-Marc Lalier with the exception of:
Bureau National Interprofessionel du Cognac pp. 4-5, p 13, p 19, p. 21 (bottom),
p. 22 (below, Alain Danvers), p. 24 (Bernard Verrax), p. 149,
D.R.: P. 11, 12, 14 (left, center and right), p. 15, 16, 17 (top and bottom),
p. 18, 20, 21(top), p. 22 (top), p. 23, 25, 31 (at left and top),
p. 39, 40, 43 (top), p. 44, 45, 46, 47, 51, 52 (top and bottom),
p. 59, 62 (at left) p. 66, 74, 75, 78, 79, 81 (top), p. 82-83, 90 (top),
p. 97 (top and bottom) p. 100, 102, 103, 106, 107, 118, 119 (top and bottom),
the two photos on page 120, 121, 123, 128-129, 129, 130-131, 131, 133,
the two photos on page 137, 143, 150, 152 (top and bottom), p. 159.